DRIVING MR. C.

William Kerley

Stage director William Kerley has several projects cancelled and needs an extra source of income. A driving job comes up, chauffeuring a retired businessman in his luxury limousine. Mr. C. is a classic English eccentric – by turns incisive, then tragi-comically deluded. He's an unreconstructed, old-fashioned gentleman with a strong selfish streak, a terrible memory and a fiery temper.

What begins as a means to earn some extra cash soon becomes a firm friendship. The author writes a regular update to Mr. C.'s son, describing their adventures. That correspondence forms the basis of this book.

***DRIVING MR. C.** will appeal to anyone who's ever had to stay patient while dealing with a difficult elderly relative – even when that means trying to pacify a tearful carer, make a mercy-dash to a pharmacy for incontinence underwear – or help a grumpy old man with a walking-stick storm out of a restaurant at snail's pace, during a Day at the Races...*

This book is an account of the quirky joys that come when we are reminded that 'All the World's a Stage' and that everyday life is full of colourful characters who, like Mr. C., are proof that real life can be way funnier than fiction.

For Bess,
(of course..)

Prologue

Ever tried? Ever failed?
No matter. Try again.
Fail again. Fail better.
Samuel Beckett

Let me begin with a confession: the story told in this book comes about as the result of failure. My own failure to make enough of a dependable living out of my freelance career as a theatre, opera and film director.

But a director's life is a gamble, often unpredictable. Just when you think the work has dried up, a chance bolt of lightning strikes, the storm breaks, exciting news floods in - and all of a sudden you're back in rehearsal – and able to pay your bills.

Offers of work are often entirely unexpected. At the beginning of this correspondence with the Clempson Family, I had no idea that, despite having made decades solely of stage work, I would be asked to direct my first feature film. Freelance life can be like that: an inspiring unsolicited invitation, but then times where there are just no projects in the diary. It's feast or famine – sometimes several jobs that, frustratingly, clash in an otherwise empty calendar, then periods between projects, acting busy - but plagued by bread-winning worries.

My wife is a freelance singer, performing in operas and concerts internationally, and working as a recording artist. She's also an excellent singing teacher - and can earn more regular money than me by deploying those talents.

We were approaching Christmas 2013 and, as we sometimes did, ended up short of funds and stressed. As a freelancer, on website, Twitter and Instagram feed - and for the benefit of professional acquaintances on Facebook – it's tempting to spin that everything is going fantastically well the whole time, *darling*. But often this is just a fragile façade.

That Christmas I really didn't know what we were going to do for cash.

Around that time the American conductor Lorin Maazel downsized his Castleton Festival. I'd been working with Maestro M. for several years, creating shows internationally - and directed dozens of operas as Resident Stage Director at his Young Artists' Program (sic) on his country estate in Castleton, Virginia. A fertile seam of work had dried up.

But the biggest blow was the cancellation of a new production of *The Barber of Seville* in Italy, at a theatre where I'd previously directed a big-budget *Carmen* with Maazel conducting. The opera house, following financial difficulties, had gone bust. I only found out a fortnight before rehearsals were due to begin, that my production was being axed. My services - and those of my assistant director, set-designer and lighting-designer - would no longer be required. I was offered a fraction of my fee as a compensation payment which, to this day, has never materialised.

Since I wasn't making him much in the way of commission, my opera agent decided to ditch me from his artists' roster. Then I was hit with a large tax bill and, being fiscally-challenged and financially overstretched, hadn't put aside enough funds to pay it. We ended up having to take out a loan to pay H.M.R.C. the money I owed them.

I was looking for something - anything - that might bring in a few quid. I thought about delivering the Christmas Post – was that still *a thing?*

Then a neighbour, whose parents had recently moved to an apartment at a rather swish 'Retirement Village' called Inglewood, in a reconstructed stately home just a mile away from our doorstep, mentioned the fact that there was a well-to-do elderly gentleman, a retired businessman called Ron, who needed the help of a driver, to drive *his* car, on outings and errands. Would my retired father-in-law, who lives nearby, be interested? No - but perhaps, out of financial necessity - I would.

I was clutching at straws really, feeling a failure. How do other directors go straight from gig to gig, generating plaudits galore - *and* seem to have no financial worries? Recently, there was an unkind penchant in the tabloid press for 'job-shaming' – seeking out soap-opera stars who had to take less glamorous work between acting jobs. Via Twitter, performer and director Kathy Burke took a journalist to task in response to a snide piece about a former leading *Eastenders* actor who had taken a post as a security guard in a shop. *'Person gets job so her kids don't starve? Good for her.'* Actor Rufus Hound tweeted too: *'No job that supports you is beneath you.'*

But humans are hard-wired to compete. Matt Haig writes that happiness equals *'never comparing yourself to anyone else'*. I read that multi-billionaire Jeff Bezos took great pleasure in what seems a rather petty victory: telling fellow billionaire Bill Gates that he wasn't available to meet on a date Gates suggested. Presumably, even way up in the stratosphere of the hyper-wealthy, you can never win quite enough little battles.

Looking jealously sideways is addictive, but ultimately pointless. However wealthy, we'll all finish our lives equally deceased. Comparing our trajectories with others can become a toxic process. Gore Vidal quipped *'it's not enough to succeed: others must fail.'* That sounds a particularly bitter counsel, but we've all, in our more uncharitable moments, felt the lure of it.

Was I just deluded in imagining that I'd one day make such a fortune I'd be beyond money worries? My aged father, however successful my theatrical career seemed, always brought me back down to earth. Having never understood the vagaries of freelance artistic life, his customary enquiry *'Got plenty of work on, son?'* was usually followed by *'maybe one day we'll see your name in lights...'*

Hope and hopelessness are never very far apart. Only recently have I started to recycle the boxes of correspondence I've hoarded for years in my loft, hoping they might come in useful to some future biographer. Anyone who works in the arts probably has a similar mindset – a mad brave mixture of enough ego to put on a performance, coupled with enough sensitivity – sometimes verging on paranoia – to be able to faithfully interpret other people's stories. Even my mentor Jonathan Miller said that what he wanted was 'a *Niagara of praise*' and wrestled with periods of deep depression. When I worked as Jonathan's assistant director on a Shakespeare play in London, I had never seen him so miserable, despite his decades as a world-famous director, as he was at his Camden Town kitchen table, poring over a series of negative newspaper reviews of our production.

But any amount of success is never quite enough, is it? Accolades and huge amounts of capital don't necessarily equal a permanent state of elation. My wife and I went backstage to see an old friend who is now a famous movie star. He was acting in a show in the West End – but in reality this meant being trapped in the basement star-dressing-room between matinee and evening performances, cooped-up and exhausted - conspiring with his co-star to find ways to exit the theatre without being mobbed by adoring fans. Asked by my wife how it really feels to be famous, he said: '*it doesn't make you nearly as happy as you think it will.*'

But envy seems unavoidable. My psychological *bête noire* has always been the super-successful Sir Sam *Bloody* Mendes. The crazy thing is that *I don't even know* Sam B. Mendes. I've only seen him in-the-flesh on two occasions. The first was years back, at the Royal Shakespeare Company, where I was starting as assistant director and having an initial induction meeting with one of their in-house producers. Sam Mendes popped his head round the door of the little office at the Barbican Theatre. He was charming, charismatic, and - *dagger-to-my-heart* – a little younger than me. Producer Vicky's eyes lit up, the way our grumpy primary school teacher used to start smiling, the moment a fellow teacher entered the classroom.

And I once saw Sam Mendes at a party, but was too shy to speak to him. I seem to recall him leaning against a wall and talking earnestly to a beautiful young actress.

Sam *Midas* Mendes, with his brilliant career, relationships and marriages with the most talented women in showbiz.

Everything he touches theatrically or cinematically turns to gold. Rich from the moment he went into partnership with producer Cameron Mackintosh and directed a West End production of *Oliver!* that played at the London Palladium for years and had countless revivals.

Some people just seem to have *it*: that star quality. *'The fame and the girl and the money, all at one sitting'*, as Philip Larkin enviously observed. I don't wish any harm to Sam Mendes – I merely use his success story to highlight a universal human penchant for futile competition. Comparisons are invariably based on a spurious equivalence. I've spent the last fifteen years of my life mainly directing opera. Sir Sam's been otherwise engaged and hasn't directed one. Yet.

Whilst I've been very lucky in both love and in my career, I still have days where I worry about money. My wife is much more of a realist – way better at planning ahead and making provision. I tend to live in hope that things will be alright - only to find that there's another cyclical fall in my fortunes.

****

But then this little driving job came up. I had no choice but to take something, *anything* that might generate a little cash. And it proved to be a rather wonderful chapter in my life. Sometimes we need to be a little vulnerable to bring out the great kindness in others, as it certainly did for me in my association with Mr. C. and his generous family.

And so I found myself, stepping into the Bistro Bar at Inglewood Retirement Village, to meet the old charmer himself, Mr. Ronald Clempson.

******

The irony of course is that reading back through the emails that make up this book, I realise *just how well* I was doing professionally in the years that I knew Mr. C. I was busy - away from home frequently – sharing the childcare with my wife around her performing schedule. I was directing plays and operas, running workshops and master-classes, making my first feature film – fortunate that my work has been both varied and fulfilling. I daresay there might even be other directors who, along the way, have been jealous of *my* career. So what if there were gaps in my schedule when I got to spend quality time with my young family? In truth, I had fallen on my feet again. Looking out for Mr. C. was a privilege Ron's family entrusted me with - and one that helped me pay the bills between rehearsal periods.

And anyway - who knows what's *really* going on in the heads of those people whose careers we covet? Shakespeare says '*there's nothing good or bad, but thinking makes it so,*' and all our lives are only as happy as the narrative we tell ourselves, and others, about our life's journey. If we can sharpen our observations, we theatricals get the chance to '*hold a mirror up to nature*'. There are stories constantly happening around us in real life, tales that might merit re-telling, characters who might prove fascinating to explore. Jonathan Miller always talked enthusiastically of shining a light on life's '*negligible details*' and drawing an audience's attention to everyday miracles we often ignore.

The producer David Puttnam once got really annoyed with the brilliant playwright and screenwriter Jack Rosenthal. Jack had told David he would be half-an-hour late for an important meeting - he needed to talk to a builder at home. At the end of the meeting Putnam drew Rosenthal aside.

PUTTNAM: (angrily) You need to talk to a builder? You've more important things to do than talk to builders! Like being on time for meetings, for example! Like writing, or filming, or thinking every second of the day! You could be the most prolific, terrific writer in Britain if you hired other people to talk to builders!

Jack was a bit shocked by the exchange. He probably *was* the most prolific writer in Britain. It was only later he thought of this reply:

ROSENTHAL: But.. it was people like builders who peopled my scripts. If I didn't talk to builders and people like builders I wouldn't have all that much to write about, and I wouldn't have written half the things I already had. Needless to say, I didn't think of this till I was in the car on the way home. To talk to a plumber.

9

All the world really is a stage - and you never know who you might meet in the wings. Old Mr. Clempson, in his often-deluded, delightful-then-demanding, self-aggrandising, King Lear-like way, was a *real* character. But for falling on challenging times financially, I wouldn't have got to meet him, and wouldn't have this story to tell.

******

And so, in the winter of 2013, I cycled down the lane to Inglewood to meet Mr. C. He was always a sharp dresser. He sat up at the zinc bar in the bistro, like some suave movie crooner, a flute of champagne at his fingertips. I introduced myself, *'Ron Clempson,'* he said, beaming an old roué's, mega-watt smile. We went up in the lift to his apartment to discuss my driving Mr. C. in his enormous, long-wheel-base limousine of an Audi – registration plate A3 OLD. Ron tapped his way along the corridor with an elegant, bone-handled cane.

Ron said I should talk to his son Graham about the details of our arrangement....

******

These emails were never meant for publication. I wrote about 650 of them in the five years that I knew Ron and pinged them off to his family. In the weeks when I was at home - not away rehearsing a show - and had spent time with Ron, on a Sunday evening I'd send his son Graham a newsletter. It was an account of Ron's welfare, our adventures that week, the hours that I'd worked, the cash Ron had spent on shopping or meals out - hoping to elicit the odd chuckle with my descriptions of Graham's father's eccentricities – but not expecting a wider audience for these words....

2013

2nd December 2013

To: Graham Clempson
Subject: Driving Mr. C

Dear Graham

Very good to speak with you.

I have talked things through with my wife & I'd be delighted to help.

I do believe I might just be able to look after your father better than one of the care-team drivers from Inglewood & give him a consistency of contact & am well-versed in topics that might interest him & pretty flexible & on the doorstep & am confident I can create a steady communication channel with you which might be currently lacking.

Do let me know what you think..

2nd December 2013 (II)

A thousand thanks.

I can send you a scanned copy of my driving licence tomorrow. (It is clean - I've never been done for speeding or had points etc - me = a staid traffic cop's son - my dear wife is the "Petrol-Head" in our family & about to do *another* speed-awareness course!)

As you suggest, I will email you weekly with scanned petrol receipts/expenses/journey details.
As appropriate I can have the car cleaned/valeted in Hungerford - I will quote you a price for this for your

approval. I will let you know if there are any mechanical issues - please let me know in due course if the car is due for a service etc.

I am self-employed as a freelance theatre director so any money you pay to me I will enter into my books as income, to give to my accountant at end of financial year.

3rd December 2013

As per your request, on the evidence of today's outing, I'm confident that I could take your Dad shopping, without the need to incur the costs of a surplus carer - if he is okay with this. (Though today he seemed to rather enjoy holding onto his young lady helper's arm...)

10th December 2013

Drove Ron to M&S at Newbury Retail Park to buy butter, yoghurt and Weetabix. In the car on way back from M&S Ron asked me if I'd be okay with shopping *without* a carer in tow. He said he'd been allocated some sub-standard carers of late who had *'made errors'*. I said I'd be content to drive as well as to offer in-store help.

12th December 2013

Medically speaking: Ron is finding getting in and out of the car quite taxing, is somewhat unsteady on his feet - but seems to be enjoying his trips out. I make sure I always come round to the passenger side to open & close car door for him. He is often out-of-breath when we arrive somewhere - or return home. But I think, as we discussed, that the freedom engendered by being able to travel in A3 OLD is giving him pleasure.

16th December 2013

Apologies for being the bearer of bad news - but I'm sorry to report that I took your dad to the Royal Berkshire Hospital in Reading today, but he decided he wanted to leave *without* having his pre-arranged C.T. scan.

Got Ron to the hospital X-Ray department quite early – about 12.20pm.

He asked me to see if there was a way of him being seen sooner – someone went off to check but no cancellations - so then I proposed that we go to the restaurant to wait for his allotted time..

The restaurant a distance away & the previous corridors & lifts had exhausted Ron so I went off in search of a wheelchair
& when I got back your Dad told me that he changed his mind
& *didn't* want to stay for the scan
& would have it done *privately* at the London Clinic
& insisted that he wanted to be taken home...
& waxed lyrical about Private Medicine versus the horrors of the N.H.S. ...

I'm afraid I really couldn't persuade him to wait - so did as I was asked & brought him back to Inglewood.

Do hope you don't think I'm being too weedy - but honestly, once Ron had made up his mind that he wouldn't stay, there seemed to be little point in trying to force him to do anything...

19th December 2013

Thanks for your reassuring words about the unexpectedly abandoned hospital visit on Monday. I do understand the situation & will do my best to help if I can...

Ron said something today about having been sent another appointment by the N.H.S. for January but I'm not sure if this is really the case. He seems to think that he'll be asking me to drive him to Harley Street in the New Year.

24th December 2013

Sorry to bother you on Christmas Eve but if there's a chance you could send me the payment for last week's driving, I'd be eternally grateful. Hope you have a great Christmas!

24th December 2013 (II)

Thanks so much Graham...

Money safely received
& much appreciated.

Merry Christmas!

2014

To: Graham Clempson
Subject: Driving Mr. C

Hi Graham

Happy New Year to you & yours!

I gather it's Ron's birthday tomorrow (is it??).
Let me know if you need any intervention from this end -
I can take him flowers or whatever if you'd like.

10th January 2014

I had lunch with your Dad yesterday at Inglewood.
He's on pretty good form - chirpily chatty with the various *female* staff as they pass by etc... the usual forgetfulness persists, of course. This evening I found him confused about the lamps in his sitting-room & trying to replace bulbs. I thought it might be a circuit tripped & investigated in a cupboard - but turned out it was just the switch on the wall which Ron had left in the off position. Problem solved.

Ron still seems keen on the idea of doing work with a physiotherapist & improving his walking speed. He's finding it hard to get in and out of the car - but I think he enjoys our trips out. He was quite *chillaxed* after a morning massage the other day...

He says that he's not happy with the hair-cutting situation at Inglewood & expressed a desire to go back to see his old barber in Henley-on-Thames & would I consider driving him there for future haircuts...?

28th January 2014

Pleased to report that your Dad's trip to Dr Laidlaw went well. Ron very relieved that his eyesight hasn't deteriorated & that he doesn't have to return for another six months. The journeys in and out of London were fine - traffic not bad at all, despite torrential rain on the way in - he was with the Doctors from 3.55pm until 5.10pm & I got him back to Inglewood for 7pm & he kindly invited me to stay for supper with him & was on good form, introducing me to his friends etc.

One piece of bad news to report - I'm really sorry - is that we came out of the London Clinic to find we had a parking ticket. I didn't tell Ron because I didn't want to worry him. My mistake entirely. I'd thought we were allowed to park on a single-yellow-line with a Disabled Badge & Time-of-Arrival-Disc prominently displayed. All the parking bays were full, but there was a short stretch of single-yellow-line right outside the Eye Clinic - a very short walk for Ron, on his unsteady feet, from car to entrance hall.

1st February 2014

Thanks SO MUCH Graham, the funds are greatly appreciated. (Just been whacked again by the bastard HMRC so this little job is a total godsend.)

10th February 2014

.... message received & understood – let me know if I can help further from this end - I'm only a 5-minute cycle ride from Inglewood. (I always find it funny when I turn up on my trusty old push-bike & then drive back out through the gates in Ron's fancy Audi!)

11th February 2014

Since I'm indisposed that day, Ron's asked me to recommend a local taxi driver for his London Clinic appointment on Monday 17th.

I'm going to recommend local taxi-driver Tracey who drives me to Heathrow sometimes. Following some recent less-than-entirely-PC comments, I checked that Ron doesn't mind a woman driver (!) & he replied *'Frankly, Will, I don't care if it's a monkey'...*

14th February 2014

Yesterday Ron decided he wanted to take a trip to Majestic Wines. I drove him to the branch in Newbury (our nearest) but, when we arrived, he produced correspondence from the Marlborough Branch & said he'd prefer to go there instead.... so we had a pleasant trip down the A4 to pick up 24 bottles of wine.

22nd February 2014

At M&S Ron decided he wanted to buy more flowers than his weekly £7.50 spray of lilies. So he bought a £3.50 bunch of yellow roses and, ever the charmer, presented it to Eve the Receptionist when we got back to Inglewood...

28th February 2014

We discussed the possibility, while I'm working away in U.S.A. for the next couple of months, of instigating some kind of 'Click & Collect' computer pre-order arrangement with M&S so that someone from Inglewood or Tracey-the-Taxi could pick up the collated shopping. Ron generally shops for similar things/amounts of things each week. I could easily make an inventory of the things he buys from M&S each week & let you have it - e.g.

Prawns with dip x2
Gem Lettuce x2
Cherry Tomatoes
Beetroot
Celery hearts
Toasting bread loaf x2
Raspberry punnet x2
Strawberry punnet x2
Bananas x7
Mini-quiche x6
Lilies (£7.50 bunch)

Semi-skimmed milk (2 x 2-pints)
Orange & Carrot juice (x4-6 - though not every week..)
Latticed apple pies x2
Peach/apricot yoghurt
Lurpak easy-spread butter
..........etc etc etc

(I could go on... & there are certain things he has more occasionally like Weetabix, breaded-cod.. marmalade... toothpaste... tissues...)

Ron doesn't quite understand the fact that we could remotely, from any computer in the world, set up or amend such a weekly order etc...

20th March 2014

Ron says he's spoken to one of the staff at Inglewood who will shop for him in her own car while I'm away. However, for some reason which was unclear to me, Ron says that the potential shopper isn't keen to go to M&S, but wants to go to a cheaper (?) supermarket....

So, this morning Ron rang to request a trip to the Tesco Superstore in Newbury so he could have a look around & judge the quality of its products etc & then I took him back to Inglewood for his lunch. After lunch Ron said he wanted to go to the (similar) Sainsbury Superstore & have a look round there - so we duly did. Ron looked very disapprovingly at these enormous, barn-like megastores...(but it was fascinating to see his property-mogul, pounds-per-square-feet brain, whirring away...)

Thanks so much for entrusting me with the challenge of Driving Mr. C. in these past weeks.
It's been a pleasure getting to know your Dad a little bit. Do feel free to take on another driver who can give you a more long-term commitment during my American absence, but I'd be happy to resume in May if that works for you & Ron.

1st May 2014

I went to Inglewood to collect a shopping list - but Ron said he'd like to come along but that he'd stay in the Audi & not come in to the shops with me.

Good that Ron wanted to come out for a change of scene - but this is the first time he hasn't wanted to venture from the car. I have the wheelchair in the car boot at all times - in case he wants to be mobile-but-sedentary.

Apart from his mobility problems however, Ron seems very chirpy, laughing a lot & generally on good form... keen to know what I think of Nigel Farage & his chances in the elections etc... Bright as a button one moment & then very confused & forgetful the next.

When I rang Ron at 12.15pm (to tell him A3 OLD's* service was complete) he said he was *only just getting up.*

*To his grown-up children's amusement – and bemusement - Mr. C's car had a personalised number plate: registration A3 OLD. Way back in his property tycoon days, he'd been persuaded by a car salesman that A3 OLD sounded like 'A FREEHOLD'. (Try saying it in your finest cockney accent.)

9th May 2014

On Tuesday Ron decided that he'd like to drive out to Lambourn - (about 15 miles away)
the village is the centre of the local horse-racing world - surrounded by various prestigious stud-farms & the high-ground above - where the horses are exercised in the early mornings... & so we duly drove there that morning for a couple of hours... though too late to see much in the way of equine-action. Nevertheless Ron greatly enjoyed the spring weather & ramping foliage & we charted a long loop around the pretty countryside & back to Fortress Inglewood...

On **Thursday** evening Ron had said he had invited a couple of friends to join him for a trip to Majestic Wines in Marlborough, where there was a wine-tasting session. Mr.

Brading, another Inglewood resident with whom Ron seems to have struck up a firm friendship had been away, staying in Buckinghamshire with his daughter & therefore hadn't received Ron's invitation.... so sent his apologies when we saw him in the entrance hall...

Jean-Claude (the chubby barman at the Inglewood Bistro) was another invitee - but when Ron went to the bar to check his whereabouts, he was informed that Thursday was Jean-Claude's day off...

So it was just Ron and myself who sped off to Marlborough and the Warehouse of Wine.

..... Ron was furious that, despite having spoken to the branch manager on the phone, there was no champagne to be tasted. He gave very short-shrift to the staff who tried to placate him....

Ron huffed & puffed but ended up buying a case of six *Perrier Jouet* & 2 bottles of *Veuve Cliquot* - but vowed he would **never** return to the accursed place & that he'd **never** known more appalling customer service etc etc...

Ron kindly invited me to stay for supper at Inglewood (he had hoped his friends would join him) & nice Mr. Brading did come and sit with us while we ate the slightly pretentious fare (pointless smears & artful flecks of sauces etc...) that they have a curious habit of presenting on wooden chopping-boards, or rough thin rectangles of Welsh slate...

Today, Ron rang early this morning & said he needed to go to Newbury's big Boots Store to investigate shaving lotions, so off we drove to the Retail Park. Having consulted one of the (rather hopeless) shop assistants, Ron decided he would take home both shaving gel *and* shaving cream in order to experiment with the best tonsorial solution.

*****

Yesterday Ron was sad to report that a close friend of his had died. Someone he said he had known since they were 12. Today, when I asked who it was, Ron was annoyed with himself that he just couldn't remember his name. Apparently, he lived in or near Salisbury - used to live in the New Forest & Ron said the funeral will be taking place in Salisbury & would I mind taking him when he found out the date..?

Of course, I'm happy to undertake this journey with your approval. But if it's a close family friend perhaps you'll be coming... Let me know...

Ron seems on good form generally - full of good humour - though less inclined to walk these days & I have to report he did ring me at 8.15am the other day in great confusion, thinking that I'd rung him (I hadn't) & suggesting that there was some fault with the phone & that it had a mind of its own & was making calls automatically...

Ron was talking today about wanting to go to the Races at Newbury Racecourse - apparently he'd had some leaflet about the numerous events that take place there - I gather he used to go there regularly, back in his Henley days...

12th May 2014

You were right - it was the late author Leslie Thomas who Ron was thinking of, though it was quite hard to prompt him: Ron was certain that his friend *wasn't* a writer etc... but then realised he *was*... poor Ron gets so frustrated by his memory problems..

I've rung Salisbury Cathedral & there is a memorial service proposed, but not yet confirmed, for 14th June & this service is open to all to attend & they've told me that the funeral is imminent, but going to be private & close family only.

If it is 14th June for Memorial Service, I'm afraid that's when I'm away directing a show in Saudi Arabia with National Youth Theatre, but I'll let you know when the date is confirmed.

16th May 2014

Ron was unhappy about the fact there's been a very loud crane working away outside his apartment- it's fixing something to do with the initially badly-installed & ill-fitting apartment windows – but this means he hasn't been able to rest in the afternoons etc.

On **Tuesday** Ron asked me to go on an errand to buy two boxes of chocolates for the women who work in the spa/treatment wing at Inglewood.

... I found Ron drinking champagne on the sunny terrace outside the bar - where he has been fleeing to escape the noise of the accursed crane which has been the bane of his week.

FRIDAY - I telephoned this morning as I do each day - usually around 10am by which time he's more *'with it'* & Ron said he might need me this afternoon - but I rang again after lunch & he sounded weary & said he needed a rest. I think the annoyance of that crane outside his window has meant he's been extra-tired this week. He'd gone down to have lunch in the bistro - fish that he said was delicious - only to find that the wretched machine had followed him - to make a racket outside the windows on *that* side of the building....

This week Ron reminisced, as far as he was able with his fugue-state memory-banks, about his friend, the best-selling author Leslie Thomas & what a good chap he was & how he'd pulled himself up from humble early beginnings as a Barnardo Boy by sheer force of personality & wit & imagination & ENERGY. Ron finds it frustrating not to be able to remember things - but is in generally good spirits, I think.

Re. possible alternative drivers from Leslie Thomas's Memorial Service: David is a friend we made at my son Thomas's nursery school (fellow parent) & he's a pilot who flies executive jets.

You probably know about such aircraft: I think he said it was a Hawker Siddley 125 (?) & David's in a transition period as he re-trains for a new Bombardier plane & so currently has a bit more time on his hands. He's been in that crazy world of flying billionaire Russian Oligarchs (& their dogs) to Nigeria & Nice - and has a regular booking from a wealthy English Duke (who - strictly *entre nous* - always makes a point of taking an aristocratic dump in the aircraft toilet just before landing. *Classy.*)

24th May 2014

On **Tuesday** morning Ron sent me out to Hungerford to get 4 boxes of Kleenex Man-Size Tissues & 2 bottles of Listerine mouthwash & in the afternoon, I took the car to the nice, efficient Albanians at Hungerford Garden Centre Car Wash.

On **Thursday** Ron decided he'd like to drive over to Henley-on-Thames & search for a thatched pub he remembered & proposed to take an old friend for lunch there on 30th & so we drove over to Henley... I consulted Google to try to find the likely hostelry & drove to a place called Pishill where there was a pub called The Crown Inn - with a thatched barn attached. Ron was insistent that this wasn't the place he had in mind.

We ended up taking a trip down memory lane & to Ron's former Henley home, Soundess House - where the electronic gates opened unexpectedly & a man who might have been the owner turned up & said Ron was welcome to come & have a look around or to return on another occasion - but Ron politely declined...

We kept exploring to try to find that thatched pub but this was rather tricky as Ron couldn't remember either its name or location. We passed several other pubs on our peregrinations but Ron said none of them were right.*

On **Friday** I went over at about 9.30am & tried to help Ron with some admin - he's getting frustrated by not being able to read his correspondence/remember his plans & says he's asked Inglewood if they could supply him with some kind of admin-helper...

Sharon, his current domestic helper, turned up & helped compile a shopping list (Ron had struggled to make his own version) & so I headed off to M&S at the Retail Park.

Ron says he'd like to investigate the possibility of sending his washing out to some kind of laundry service in the vicinity, as he says he used to do in London & isn't happy with the system at Inglewood where someone does his washing (I assume in the machine in his apartment) but he finds this inexpert & unsatisfactory & some garments have shrunk in the process. I can find out if there is such a collection & delivery service in the area...

..... With my daughter Louisa (3) we found Ron in the restaurant eating a luminous orange soup. He was utterly enchanted with little Louisa, asked the waiter to bring her a bowl of ice-cream & chatted away merrily to her & when I took Louisa for a walk in the gardens & reported to Ron that we'd seen the swimming pool, Ron said that she (and her brother) must come as his guests & swim in the Inglewood pool. Later in the week he was adamant that he wanted to buy Louisa and Thomas some armbands & floats & swimming accessories & insisted I took the cash from him which he pressed into my hand.

I later found out why we couldn't find that thatched pub in Henley. The pub in question was actually the Cott Inn at Dartington in South Devon – 180 miles away and remembered from a different part of Ron's life.

31st May 2014

I took Ron to Hungerford to meet Mr. Barnaby Smith at Caviste - an Independent Wine Dealer whom, pleased to report, Ron took to immediately. Though he did say that his name *sounded American.. (?)*

.... This week I made three journeys on personal business. Two to my mother's house (58 miles away) - my father is suffering ever-worsening dementia & it's great to try to be more present at this horrid stage... & one to Barnes SW13 (62 miles away) in order to pick up the John Piper picture & books I have been left by Basil Coleman - he was a close

24

friend in his later years - an important mentor of mine - he died at the age of 96 last year.

(Basil was the original director of Benjamin Britten's operas TURN OF THE SCREW, GLORIANA, LET'S MAKE AN OPERA and BILLY BUDD & his estate have approached me to write his biography - a massive task. I now need to find some funding for the research stages which will take me a couple of years as I don't have any income if I'm not directing plays/operas/working with organisations like the National Youth Theatre (or driving Ron!). All very daunting but an immense privilege.... despite writing Basil's obituary for *The Guardian* & giving the main address at his funeral etc - I've never written a biography before so... GULP!!

Basil's centenary is in 2016 & there's going to be an exhibition about his work at the Red House Library in Aldeburgh.

.... like your dad, I am now the proud owner of a John Piper print! I've noticed one on his wall at Inglewood - though he doesn't remember its provenance - though, of course, John & Myfanwy Piper lived near Henley at Fawley Bottom.

Pleased to report that Ron has already had a delivery of two cases of wine from Caviste in Hungerford - has sampled the contents and pronounced Barnaby-the-Wine-Dealer an excellent find. *Phew...*

Health-wise - this time Ron walked round M&S, didn't stay in the car (I always scoot off with the trolley to get the stuff) & he was very out-of-breath at the end of our shop.
I always offer to take Ron in the wheelchair but he's reluctant to use it... I'm not sure how much longer this will be possible.

He was also stunned by the depth *of his own* confusion - when I said that Tony, the stand-in driver would be in touch with you re. motor insurance Ron said *'Yes - best if he talks to* **my Dad'** & then amazed that he'd said **'dad'** instead of **'son'** & then got tragically confused
& said *'but who is my Mum? I don't know where my mum is'* & it took a while to calm him down

& I suggested that confusing the titles of close male relatives was an easy thing to do & that his parents were surely in a better place & all was well etc.. etc...

The tricks Ron's memory (or lack of it) are playing on him are hard for him to deal with - but I try to gently reassure him - even if this means repeating the same thing several times & on consecutive telephone calls & days...

ON a lighter note - we spent the swimming fund that Ron kindly gave to my children on some floats & goggles & rubber rings - he was delighted when I told him....

... it now turns out we are not permitted to use the pool at Inglewood because we are not family members - but Ron says he wants to sort this out for us to swim as his guests.
So, you see, Ron's kindness endures & his great sense of humour too - even if his failing memory continues its turbulent trajectory...

6th June 2014

Oh God, Graham - I'm SO sorry
Yes, that must have been *me* driving
Argh - massive apologies - I'm *very* embarrassed
Please let me know how I can pay the speeding fine...

I'm writing this from a very long queue at immigration trying to get into Saudi Arabia for my NYT work..

Again mega-apologies for inconveniencing you. I've never had a speeding ticket before - my wife had had a couple & has done speed awareness course & I've been smug about my previous clean record - so *serves me right...*

I owe you an email about driving Ron this week - I took him to a wine-tasting yesterday & he seemed to enjoy it..

8th June 2014

Asalam alaykum from my sojourn in Al Hasa with the NYT... we've started our drama workshops with 25 local lads & all is well but quite a challenge culturally...

26

Last week in summary:

MONDAY

Ron kindly invited me to lunch with him & his friend Mr. Brading. They sit grandly at table in their high-backed leather chairs, like old Garrick Club members... Their memories are both rather challenged. It was like dining with the John Gielgud and Ralph Richardson characters from that Pinter play full of surreal *non-sequiturs* entitled NO MAN'S LAND...

Ron has kindly given Mr. Brading one of his walking-sticks. Mr. Brading constantly kept forgetting that Ron had made a present of the stick.

                        BRADING/RICHARDSON:

Is that your stick?

                        CLEMPSON/GIELGUD:

What?

                        BRADING/RICHARDSON:

The stick. [pause] It belongs to you, does it?

                        CLEMPSON/GIELGUD:

No.

                        BRADING/RICHARDSON:

Yes. That's your stick.

                        CLEMPSON/GIELGUD:

But I've just given it to you, Peter! Ha! Ha!

                        BRADING/RICHARDSON:

No. It's yours. It looks like one you'd use. [Pause] Have you given it to me?

                        CLEMPSON/GIELGUD:

What? What's that, John?

[CLEMPSON consistently forgets BRADING'S first name.]

BRADING/RICHARDSON:
Have we ordered?

ME:
Yes, gents, I think, you both chose the
haddock...

CLEMPSON/GIELGUD:
Did we?

BRADING/RICHARDSON:
The haddock. Ah, yes. Ha! Ha! The
haddock, you say! [taps menu] Shall we
order, then?

CLEMPSON/GIELGUD:
[examining his own walking stick as if for
first time]
Is that your stick, Peter?

etc etc...

WEDNESDAY
Ron rang in state of high agitation having spilt coffee down
his trousers
& could I possibly take them to dry-cleaners immediately
because the care staff at Inglewood are all a bunch of idiots
& the place is generally ridiculous
& the management a gang of morons
& he's decided he's going to have to sell the apartment etc..
but I managed to calm him down as best as I could..
& took away the trousers...

THURSDAY
Ron and I looked into fridge & cupboards & compiled a list
of groceries because his current helper Sharon, who usually
writes a weekly, (semi-literate), shopping list wasn't around
this week.

Ron has decided he will **never** order lilies again because as
he brushes past them
they stain his shirts with pollen & nobody bloody tells him &
he can't see...

28

& therefore I bought him some roses instead.

Evening - took Ron to wine-tasting at Chilton Lodge on massive local country estate
beyond Hungerford. Full of local toffs quaffing & pontificating about grape varieties & vintages - Ron seemed to enjoy it - particularly when a rather glamorous *lady-of-a-certain-age* with a remarkable cleavage parked herself on the sofa next to him, chatting away...
She wanted to know all about what it's like to live at Inglewood etc.. etc... they exchanged cards because she'd love to see his apartment *for a friend* who's interested in buying one etc..

This event was at the invitation from local wine merchants called Caviste - I took Ron to see Barnaby in the branch in Hungerford last week & Ron made an order for two cases & seems to like them & found the wine delicious & thinks Barnaby & Caviste a very good thing & a world away from those charlatan box-shifters at Majestic Wines...

13th June 2014

All goes well with NYT in Saudi Arabia - making a show with a wonderful group of local young men & it's great to bring a team of NYT members out here for their first experience of working in this way though culturally it's tricky - the religious police really don't approve of theatre or music - so it's all very undercover & we may get shut down at any point... in fact, word got out about the parallel course with local women
& the oil company who is sponsoring the project got cold feet & closed it down...

Prayer times are sacrosanct, everything shuts & you never see a woman who isn't wearing a full black *abaya* (including face covering...) quite something... though I gather that most weekends many rich young people storm over the causeway to Bahrain, rip off their burqas (revealing (revealing) bikinis) & get hammered....

I'm not much of a drinker myself, but I must say a *proper* cold beer will go down a treat on my return to Blighty... the alcohol-free lagers on offer here are pretty dire.... but what

I'm most missing, here in the desert, is the lovely GREEN aspect our *"Green and Pleasant Land"*...

Thank *Allah* for Air-Con

27th June 2014

Ron said that Tony (who drove him & Maggie to the Leslie Thomas Memorial Service while I was away) was an okay driver. But a bit slow.. (*haha!*)

On **Wednesday** I drove Ron to the menswear department of Newbury's Camp Hopson department store. He had been looking at a catalogue of an online/mail order clothing company & talked about visiting their stockists in Windsor (46 miles away). Camp Hopson is altogether closer to home (8 miles) & his friend Mr. Brading (he of the surreal lunchtime Pinter one-act plays) buys his togs there...

At Camp Hopson Ron tried on & then chose two pairs of trousers. The hems need to be taken up & I think I heard Ron asking for the seams to be narrowed too...

On **Friday** (today) Ron's new trousers were ready for collection from Camp Hopson so I drove into Newbury to collect them. He hasn't tried them yet so I'm not sure if the trousers/alterations will meet with his approval. He certainly thought they were tremendously good value for a couple of pairs of slacks. (I think he was making a comparison with Savile Row prices...)

I rang Ron after lunch & he said that he'd got the name of a laundry called *Thames Valet* (sic.) Laundry Services *(see what they did there?)* - who would pick up from Inglewood & re-deliver..

As previously reported, Ron's been complaining for a while about how unsatisfactory the system is at Inglewood & how his best shirts get ruined etc..
& so he asked me to come to Inglewood immediately - because we urgently needed to drive to the laundry's HQ near Wallingford, Oxon, with a bag full of Ron's dirty laundry...

& so it came to pass that we journeyed for 30 miles, in stop-start Friday late-afternoon traffic, to an industrial unit just outside Wallingford, where Ron handed over his laundry and paid in cash. Apparently the laundry will be delivered to him at Inglewood on Tuesday. He seems to think that now there'll be a service that will take away his dirty washing & deliver it clean etc...

3rd July 2014

... tomorrow I'm off to London for a meeting with the Chief Executive of Opera Philadelphia which I'm hoping is going to result in a major new production for me to direct (the U.S. premiere of a new opera which had its European premiere in 2012). Fingers crossed... (everything crossed!).. of course he might have offered to take me to lunch to commiserate & say how sorry he is that he's offered the gig so some other bloody director... this time tomorrow I will know...

MONDAY

8.30am Ron rang me in a state of high agitation saying that it was *an emergency.*
The trousers he bought & had altered were quite the wrong length & could I come to Inglewood with a tape measure immediately?

Bought a tape measure in Hungerford & took it to Inglewood where we established that the alterations done on the trousers, subsequent to purchase, were unsatisfactory (by a whole 2 inches) & so we returned to Camp Hopson menswear department & Ron tried the trousers on again & showed the staff how short they were & they pinned them up & took another payment from him (!) with the promise that they would get it right this time...

THURSDAY

Ron has had some dental discomfort & had a Hungerford dentist recommended by another Inglewood resident. I took him there for a 3pm appointment. His mouth looked pretty sore - but he said there was no pain. I urged him to rest & tried to find out if he had Paracetemol etc. He asked me to go to Boots and buy him new toothbrushes with soft bristles (paid cash).

31

Ron was insistent yesterday that I should meet with understudy driver Chris & train him how to go shopping at M&S - *'so there will be no excuses'*.

*****

Ron hasn't shown any interest in going for a food-shop this week. I think he's been taking all his meals in the bistro - but I'm not entirely sure. He said the staff weren't available to make a shopping list. I have offered to do the same as last week & examine cupboards & fridge & draft the list with him.   Last week I noticed that several things in the fridge (raspberries etc) were going mouldy & had to be discarded - so I'm not sure what's happening in terms of the housekeeping...

..... Ron was in high dudgeon today about the idiotic way the café/restaurant is being run at Inglewood & how the dratted cranes which are fixing the window are going to ruin the use of the terrace & how the terrace café tables should be relocated further up the lawn terraces but the management are a bunch of morons etc & the poor staff much put-upon by the managers who are brainless idiots & have no idea how much money they are going to lose if the crane-deployment interferes so drastically with the restaurant trade & the possibilities for *al fresco* dining etc etc...

Ron always seems chirpier after a good blast at the hopeless inadequates who run Fortress Inglewood. Today he stated his belief that there's some vast conspiracy going on - that *dark forces* are at work behind the scenes & that there's much corruption and cronyism festering ... all very dramatic....

Ron said he was going to interview someone this week to be his secretary (?!) - a friend of Mandy - one of the Inglewood staff.... I haven't heard the result of this...

On the laundry front: Ron told me that his clothes had been successfully delivered by Thames Valet Laundry Co. & that they were wonderfully well done... Just like the old days, he says & he intends to continue to use their services...

4th July 2014

Ron rang me about 8.40pm in a state of great confusion - not knowing if it was day or night - sounding very muddled - should he be getting ready for bed or getting up? - I think the light evening adding to his befuddlement - said he'd fallen asleep & woken up not knowing where he was...

I offered to cycle down to Inglewood - but he said he'd be fine - I reassured him the disorientation could be a bi-product of the anaesthetic from his dental treatment - I think he had a wisdom tooth extracted & dentist will have given him a fair dose of painkiller... Really he needed someone there to look after him.. I did offer to return but he was insistent I shouldn't go back & he'd get ready for bed etc...

I will ring Ron in a bit & check he's okay - but you or another family member might want to give him a call & check how he is today..

.... Just rang Ron & he sounds fine - district nurse had a look at him & says all well. He didn't sleep too well but says mouth healing & not in discomfort - good news –

5th July 2014

Thanks so much for prompt remuneration & reimbursement - so much appreciated & unlike my directorial career where contracts take forever to pay & my agent is always having to hassle! Much appreciated!

14th July 2014

Do hope all is well with you & Emma. Sorry this missive is a little later than my customary *Confessions of a Country Chauffeur*..

Last week I was away on a research trip in Aldeburgh on Monday and Tuesday so the Audi was at Inglewood & my deputy Chris was standing by, but Ron didn't decide to use him....

33

I rang Ron on Wednesday morning & when he heard that it was my Claire's birthday & I was taking her out for lunch, Ron kindly said that I should have the rest of the day free & he wouldn't avail himself of my driving services... Claire drove her car to the pub
& I pushed the boat out with a lunchtime pint-and-a-half of shandy.

Oh yes, we really are *Livin' the Dream* down here in West Berks...

Thursday - took the Audi for a mini-valet care of the kindly Albanians at Hungerford Garden Centre Car Wash.

Apparently having had no-one to help him do so - Ron had made his own shopping list. Ron decided he didn't want to walk around the shops so I scooted off with the trolley leaving him in the car. Ever affirmative, Ron kindly said that I would take '*any existing prize for speed-shopping....*'

Friday - Emergency! Ron said he'd failed to add bananas to his shopping list & would I bring him some. He cheered up when I asked him to sing '*Yes, we have no Bananas!*' - but said he couldn't '*sing falsetto...*' (?!)

When I arrived at his apartment Ron was eating lunch there with one of the staff-members having prepared it & she was busy hoovering around him.. so that apartment-service evidently still continues - despite the fact Ron often complains there's so little assistance & the place is going to rack & ruin etc etc...

FYI: I have paid that wretched speeding fine of £100
& sent off both parts of my licence for the application of 3 penalty point black marks...
Mea maxima culpa....

My wife is greatly amused by my Fall from Motoring Grace...

On **Saturday** 19th, Ron has asked me to take him to Newbury Racecourse.
There's a Berry Brothers (a firm he seems to like) wine-tasting at 11am & then a race meet thereafter. Despite a

West-London-childhood spent walking our dogs around the perimeter fence of Kempton Park, I have never actually been to The Races before - so I'm intrigued to find out what it's all about. Since he has a blue Disabled Badge, I have free admission as Ron's 'carer'.

Ron says he met a woman last week to talk to her about becoming some sort of 'secretary' - he said he was glad to meet her but not sure she's the right person etc...
(I have no further casting-couch information to give you about this secret audition...)

I'm not sure if you'd like me to look into getting Ron registered disabled with West Berkshire Council for A3 OLD (someone told me last week it stood for *A Freehold??* – in tribute to Ron's days in the property business - I had wondered...)

As previously stated: my next period of absence is when I'm directing Peter Maxwell-Davies' CINDERELLA in Scotland with Cromarty Youth Opera & I'll be away from 28th July until 16th August. I've already primed Chris with these dates & he's said he can understudy for me one the *Driving Mr. C* front...

15th July 2014

Ron was a trifle agitated today by the fact that his new laundry service had delivered but not collected his washing this week. He rang me at 8.30am to ask me to pick up this week's washing & take it the 29 miles to Wallingford... which I duly did....

When I got there they were apologetic but said their driver had knocked & knocked at the door of Ron's apartment & they'd rung & rung from H.Q. but to no avail....

I've given them alternative phone numbers & told them they probably need to push the door open & shout **"MR. CLEMPSON"** if they want to make sure of Ron hearing.. The good news is that Ron continues to seem very pleased with the laundry service offered by Thames Valet Laundry Services... shirts perfectly pressed etc...

20th July 2014

On **SATURDAY** the Great Day had arrived - we were off to Newbury Races! Ron kindly lent me a pair of his old binoculars. I arrived at Inglewood at about 10am - Ron in a bad mood about the weather being so changeable & visibility bad & we wouldn't be able to see *a bloody thing* - but in due course we arrived at the Racecourse for the Berry Brothers' wine-tasting - a lecture from one of their representatives & then some wines to taste. Ron only tried one *sauvignon blanc* & then said we should go & find some lunch.

Jessica, the membership secretary, informed us that the Hennessy Restaurant, (the nearest to fine-dining the racecourse affords), was full & we wouldn't be able to get a table there. She said there was a brasserie (though with no view of the course), though Ron wasn't keen on this option... or, she suggested, we go up into the Members' Boxes - in another building & on third floor - but, after an epic struggle to get up there, this was a rather cramped & run-down affair, not to Ron's liking, where the only dining options were mere cold-collations.

Moving from building to building of course is very difficult and slow for poor Ron. He hangs onto my arm & we snail-pace along. Despite being initially marshalled to the wrong car-park etc... I managed to get the car parked as close to the entrance as possible - but it's still a distance through the gate & to the stands etc. But Ron still adamant that he doesn't want to use the wheelchair, so we just took our time & I carefully watch him lest (heaven forfend!) he falls...

Finally, I left Ron on the ground floor of the first building we'd entered & took the lift to the Hennessy Restaurant to see if there was any chance of getting a table - if anyone had cancelled. Ron also said I should try offering them a financial inducement to make this possible & entrusted me with his wallet. At the restaurant it was no-go - they said that people pay £150 in advance for their meals - so that no-one ever cancels. I sportingly offered them a *Clempson Bung,* but there was no swaying them.

36

The whole place was becoming ever more packed as more trains & coaches & hundreds of cars arrived, bearing rowdy race-goers. Ron seemed to think that *'the world and his wife'* were there & that it was a totally different class of folk to the ones he'd been accustomed to meeting elsewhere - e.g. at Royal Ascot...

In truth: Ron was not best pleased with his first modern experience of Newbury Racecourse. Surely we could have been informed that it was imperative to book in advance if one wanted to eat in the classiest of the eateries etc etc...?

The first race was due to start at 1.05pm but, sorry to report, we didn't see any racing yesterday at all - Ron decided that it was all a bit of a disaster & that if we couldn't eat in comfort & watch the racing then what was the point?

& we should just get out of this hell-hole & was there a pub I could recommend for a nice lunch nearby?

I tried to persuade Ron that we might be able to find some compromise - there was a rather natty seafood bar/should I go and investigate the brasserie? - but your dear Dad was adamant & so we were off....

I have learnt there's no gainsaying him once Ron's made up his mind...

So, against the oncoming tide of loud-mouthed proletariat punters, we worked our laborious progress back through the turnstiles & to the car & out of the muddy car park & whizzed past the traffic jams backed up all the way through the Newbury Ring Roads & back out on the A4 towards Hungerford - with me racking my brains for a restaurant a disgruntled Mr. C. might find acceptable...

I was thinking of the Carnarvon (sic) Arms, a pub taken over by one of those shouty French/Mancunian chefs & which is raved about... but I remember seeing a picture of the decor & thinking it might not be right & that it looked a bit pokey with the tables too close together...

But then - BINGO! - I remembered The Vineyard - a 5* hotel in Stockcross, with a classy restaurant just a tiny detour from our journey back to Fortress Inglewood. Claire and I spent the first couple of nights of our honeymoon there, in those pre-children days, when we could even pretend to afford such extravagances...

So Ron & I rocked up to the front of the hotel - there seemed to be a wedding reception going on - photographs outside the bijou & *chi-chi* designer-lake at the front - so it looked busier than it was - but the restaurant was happy to accommodate us & so I brought Ron in & then a charming waitress called Rebecca took his arm
& led him to our table while I went & found a proper parking space for A3 OLD....

& when I got back, Ron was happily installed in a rather nice secluded area of the restaurant, almost like a private dining room, or a theatre box, looking down on other tables in the atrium & from this vantage point, Ron could see outside to the nuptial goings-on, as the happy couple & their nearest & dearest struck the poses to be pasted into an album & handed down the generations...

Ron had much to say about the skimpy shortness of the bridesmaids' dresses, in that way that, despite his blindness, his visual acumen suddenly ramps up when slim female company hoves into view...

Ron seemed to like this place The Vineyard immediately. (What a relief after the debacle that was our damp squib of a Day at the Races...)

The Vineyard has a wine-cellar of 30,000 bottles to choose from - at table they give you a wine encyclopaedia & the Real French Sommeliers wear their great learning with a garrulous gravitas... it is their pleasure to recommend the perfect wine to go with your guinea-fowl terrine & your *Duck-Breast-with-Vegetable-Squiggles*...

Ron was in his element & I was very fortunate to be treated to a delicious (albeit over-artfully-presented) lunch. I didn't have the heart to tell Ron that this place was one of the late Michael Winner's out-of-town favourites. It's part of that up-market Relais & Chateaux group - you know - the ones with the bible-like White Handbook - most of them (though not this one) seem to boast lawns with helipads...

Though Ron, in his perceptive way, said that in his experience, membership of what I had thought was a select club was no great guarantee of consistent quality...

We chatted away merrily of this and that & Ron seemed very pleased with both food & service after that *appalling* racecourse...
Phew!

Ron kindly gave me advice about my book (that biography of Basil Coleman (Benjamin Britten's favourite director) I am trying to raise money to research & publish) & Ron said I needed to be way more *entrepreneurial* & far less *artistic* if I was to turn it into something that would sell & something people would get on board to help me fund.... that I needed advice from a proper literary agent (which I do) & to work out why my project is unique
& who the competition are & who are my likely buyers & sponsors etc etc... in short: to formulate some sort of proper Business Plan for the work in hand...

Ron really is extraordinary company in this way, he'll have these moments of astonishing perspicacity, where I can see what a brilliant businessman he must have been - but then somehow his thoughts will curdle
& he'll begin to lace his insights with surreal references
& become confused, start overusing words like *'scenario'*
& go intellectually off-piste & deviate from logic as we know it & conversation soon takes a less comprehensible turn
& his counsel becomes rather more impenetrably esoteric...

This is tough to witness & must be so hard for you, his family who love him best & at these times I think of Shakespeare & that sad line in Hamlet *'O what a noble mind is here o'erthrown...'*

But Ron's kindness to me, even in his moments of confusion, is always strong & I appreciate it very much. *Old Boy,* he calls me: a title I take as a Badge of Honour. What a dear man he is & what a long way he has come from his boyhood in Bounds Green.

Inside the Audi: Ron's been getting very angry with his seatbelt & saying that it needs to be examined by the mechanics at Audi. There's nothing wrong with it & I've taken to gently helping him to plug it in.

Medical: Ron had a mark on the back of his right-hand where he'd cut or grazed himself & on our shopping day, he somehow took the scab off & bled down his trousers & onto the car-seat - but wiped the blood away with his hankie & most certainly didn't want me to drive him home or get out the First-Aid kit.

I don't think it's anything serious - but just so you know...

******

This week, on the car's dashboard, a warning light appeared, asking me to refill the screen-wash. With each subsequent ignition, the computer hectored me to get on and do something about it. So, screwing my courage to the sticking place, I spent £6.99 on a ready-made bottle of the stuff & devotedly read the Audi manual & opened the bonnet for the first time & as I'm no mechanic, amazed myself by finding the right hole & glugging that blue cocktail down it.

There's a rather a big engine in there...

25th July 2014

Popped in to see Ron at Inglewood with Louisa (aged 3)
& he's always very kind to her & very animated when she's around. She wanted to show Mr. Clempson her cycling helmet etc (she rides on a special seat on the back of my bike).

Ron's trousers were a little stained with food etc today & I took the liberty of gently telling him so & that it might be best to change into a clean pair. He's been cross in the past when people haven't informed him that his jumper is food-stained because he can't see & therefore doesn't know & complained to me that people are too frightened to tell him that he needs to change his cardigan etc.

40

22nd August 2014

re. that medical appointment on 15th September you wanted me to attend when I told Ron about it & wanted to write it in his diary: Ron became agitated & said it's a bunch of foreign doctors who aren't real doctors - not *'blue-blooded British'* Doctors & that they're all after drugs that they're criminally prescribing (or something)...

I'm afraid another one of his conspiracy theories kicking-in here & I couldn't quite understand his objection - but just to let you know he's resistant to that home visit of Dr Cresswell you told me about & at which you requested my presence....

Today Ron asked me to get him some after-shave - *"the stuff I put on my face after shaving."* I checked at the apartment exactly what he meant & it was actually Johnson's Baby Lotion - which I duly delivered to him.

30th August 2014

It's been a largely uneventful week - have gently continued to try to persuade your Dad that the doctor's visit on 15th September is not part of some grand conspiracy by bogus "foreign" doctors who are after our British Pharmaceuticals... Tried to tell him it's Dr Cresswell, whom I think you said he's liked before... & he asked, among his conversational non-sequiturs, *'is it that good-looking one?'*

Ron's been sitting in his window & watching the comings & goings of the heavy earth-moving vehicles opposite which are caked in mud - I think the end result is some sort of landscaped garden. Ron insisted they were also going to build a petrol filling station... (?!) He seems to think the workers are shirkers & start too late & knock off excessively early...

Out of the blue: Claire's just been cast as a chorus member in a Warner Bros blockbuster Hollywood film - so went off this week to Watford for a bespoke fitting for a fabulous gown & mask & headdress - the movie world being so prodigal - they're spending a fortune on one action scene in which our action-hero, little Tom Cruise, is pursued across the Royal Opera House stage during a performance of

TURANDOT & a gunfight ensues among the divas... they're building *a whole opera house* on a studio sound stage - for them, money is no object...

Quite the contrary for my autumn show - living off scraps doing a different Puccini opera at the Royal Academy of Music on a college budget - with countless calls to production managers to see what we have to cut next from our inexpensive set & costume design...
But I love working with young singers & we have bags of energy & collective imagination to make up for the lack of resources...

6th Sept 2014

Ron reports that a neighbour called Maggie (I think he means his ex-wife but this was unclear)* has been helping him to sort out his kitchen & has evidently tried to teach him how to make tea in a mug rather than using his unorthodox method of deploying kettle as a teapot & boiling water with teabags already floating therein (!).

Actually, I made him a cup of tea in his Grandad mug yesterday & he's astonished by this quite revolutionary approach...

Ron's railing against A3 OLD's seatbelt again – insisting that it needs attention from Audi specialists.. (I think this is incorrect & have taken to tactfully reaching across his chest & clicking seatbelt into slot...)

This week I haven't mentioned Doctor Cresswell's impending visit.. for fear of provoking a further rant about **'bogus foreign quacks'** etc... but will mention it nearer the time & remind him it's that (lady) doctor he likes & be discreetly in attendance...

Ron was married to Maggie for seventeen years before they divorced. She went on to marry a Mr. Sharp. When her second husband died, Maggie moved to Inglewood, to live in the apartment on the floor above Ron's.

12th *Sept 2014*

Yesterday evening I took Ron and your stepmother Maggie to that Caviste Wine-Tasting at nearby Richens Lodge. When I arrived at Inglewood to collect them, they were drinking champagne together in Ron's apartment. Ever charitable, Ron asked if I'd join - but I left them to it & waited with the car outside Inglewood Reception.

After the wine-tasting, Ron decided he wanted to return to The Vineyard (that 5* hotel & restaurant at Stockcross we visited on that abortive Newbury Race Day) for dinner .

I was kindly included - though things were a little stressy: the atmosphere between the two of them seemed progressively to become somewhat strained...

Maggie was keen to tell me that she thinks Alex Salmond is a bare-faced liar
& that Scotland is full of treacherous Eastern European immigrants who will vote 'YES' in the referendum next week
& that she's sick of hearing about it & of all the relentless recent media saturation
& that we've been subsidising the perfidious Scots for years (beforehand she'd checked that I'm not Scottish – I was too timid to tell her that my wife Claire was born there..)

& Maggie waxed lyrical about the merits of Sarah Vine (a.k.a. Mrs M. Gove), Quentin Letts, Richard Littlejohn & the other colourful columnists of her beloved *Daily Mail*.

She told me about life at Soundess House in Henley, when she and Ron were still married
& the day she gave clandestine safe haven, at the coach house, to singer Adam Faith - who was conducting a fleeting affair with the American tennis-star, Chris Evert. (I have just checked the saintly Daily Mail website. It was actually a two-year affair. *So now we know.)*

Maggie spoke lovingly of the ballet & opera & missing being able to easily visit Covent Garden & the National Theatre, as she could with her last, post-Ron, husband Mr. Sharp - in the good old days when they had an Oxford Street *pied-a-terre*. She reminisced about the delights of watching old-fashioned Grand Opera in that famous outdoor amphitheatre in Verona - only marred by having to fly from Gatwick in the summer - a proletarian airport full of irritating young families.

Maggie told me she'd wept when she'd heard that Pavarotti had died.

I don't think she agreed with me that he had rather limited acting skills & that it was regrettable that the *mis-en-scene* of any show had to be designed around the inevitable inertia of his massive bulk. (I didn't tell her that Pavarotti, at any performance, whatever character he was playing, had to have substantial snacks pre-set all around the stage. Neither did I tell her how glad I am that the days of such dinosaur-divas are over.)

Oh & I think I heartily disappointed her when I said that Benjamin Britten (1913-1976) is my favourite composer - his *ouevre* (he wrote his first opera PETER GRIMES over seventy years ago) - is *way too modern* for Maggie's liking.

Maggie did finally clarify for me how many children Ron has & who-is-twinned-with-whom - about which I've always been embarrassingly unclear as Ron, sadly, never seems to fully recall. Recently he told me that he was *quite certain* that none of his offspring were twins...

But then he again assured me that his late friend Leslie Thomas (bestselling author of *The Virgin Soldiers et al*) had never been a writer.

Ron, though chirpy on arrival at The Vineyard, comfortable on a sofa before the fireplace, with a glass of pre-dinner *Taittinger*; spoke seldom once we were seated at our restaurant table.

I don't think he liked the place nearly as much this time - service was slow & the music - Ella Fitzgerald - too loud (I asked the staff to unplug the speaker nearest our table) & Ron became ever more taciturn, sombre & prickly & despite ordering the four-course menu, didn't want a dessert & wanted to leave soon after the diminutive meat-course... (though we still didn't leave till after 11pm)

44

****

Last weekend I used the car for two longer-distance personal journeys, the first to my parents' house (57 miles from Kintbury) & the second, on Sunday, to Clement Danes in The Strand where Claire was *depping* in the choir at that Royal Air Force Church where Margaret Thatcher's body recently Lay in State (67 miles away).

(Claire's currently singing Handel in Leipzig & so I'm doing Daddy-Day-Care duty for three nights.)

I start rehearsals at the Royal Academy on 13th October for a few weeks of Puccini.
My stand-in-driver, Eloquent Chris is primed, ready to understudy for me & up to speed as this text testifies:

"hi will yes no problem mate its in my diary thankyou cheers"

15th Sept 2014

Sorry to report Doctor Cresswell didn't show. She'd had trouble getting to Inglewood past the road-closure...

Workmen are resurfacing Templeton Road & this has messed up access - I managed to get around the road-block - but only after following diversion & going around the other way & finding that closed & then returning to try again (a right palaver)...

I'm sorry not to be reporting better news & hope the appointment can be rescheduled soon.

Ron of course grumpy about this & sees it as another sign of medical incompetence *"they couldn't find a snail in a bloody pit"* (?!) was his gnomic conclusion...

20th Sept 2014

Ron rang early this morning to say that Monday's appointment with Dr Cresswell is not remotely convenient & would I please ring & defer it by at least a fortnight & that he doesn't want appointments at lunchtime

& that he's under the London Clinic doctors so doesn't need other incompetent doctors coming to his home
& is prepared to see doctor at surgery during normal office hours etc

Am happy to postpone or cancel on his behalf...

21st Sept 2014

I'll keep this brief because I've cut the end of my index finger on a broken bottle that I was trying to wrap in cardboard to save the dustman's hands from such an injury (chizz) and typing is annoyingly impeded...

(I usually touch-type & pretty quickly - one of the only really useful skills I learned in my teens..)

Monday you know about - waiting around for Doc Cresswell who didn't show because of that resurfacing road-block with an increasingly irate Ron shouting about charlatans & incompetents etc etc...

Wednesday - Ron rang early to say that there'd been a disastrous cock-up with his laundry collection & would I immediately drive the 54-mile round-trip to the laundry at Wallingford & deliver his dirty laundry? The nice apologetic folk there said the driver had again knocked & shouted at Ron's door but couldn't get an answer & was worried he might still be asleep...

22nd Sept 2014

Just spoke to your dad who was actually sounding in very good spirits (though a bit tired) because he'd had a lovely weekend seeing family..

He told me doc had cancelled but sounds sanguine about it... No raging against the infernal quacks this time...

27th Sept 2014

This week Ron told me on the phone that he had a *new mobile*. I got ready to take down the number & then realised that actually he meant a walking-frame which your sister Sarah-Jane has given him!

Just thought I'd let you know that the nurse offered Ron a 'flu injection but he was adamant that he didn't want that. She asked several times to no avail...

When we were in the car later I gently asked if he was sure but Ron was definitely decided against it. Just wondered if you think he needs persuading that it's a good idea to have that 'flu jab? Because he's elderly (& because he has diabetes?) he must be in one of the recommended groups. (I'm mildly asthmatic so I'm on the list.) It seems to be something doctors advocate. Ron said he'd never had it & didn't want it. But I don't know whether he really should. I'll leave it with you.

Ron was confused that morning because his domestic helpers had said they couldn't find his clean bedding. I telephoned that Laundry he uses in Wallingford to check if they had any of Ron's bedding, they didn't. I searched through his cupboards & found clean pillow cases & duvet covers & fitted sheets etc so left them on a chair for the helpers to change his bed linen. Ron very pleased that they'd been found & cursing the staff as a bunch of incompetents etc...

Ron kindly invited me to stay for lunch in the restaurant. Talked to him & his friend Mr. Brading about motorcycles they'd owned & their favourite London restaurants (neither could remember any of the names so I did a lot of guesswork) in another one of those elliptical, Pinteresque conversations..

On **Saturday** took the car for a mini-valet from the nice Albanians at Hungerford Garden Centre & thence with my Thomas (6) & Louisa (3) to see Ron in his apartment. He's particularly kind to the children & lights up when he sees them - always a pleasure
& he's very kind & his pensive mood lifts - we'd arrived in a sudden shower
& there was a rather beautiful & extensive rainbow & that was a cause of great excitement
among the elderly, the young & of course, *yours truly* in the

middle....

27th Oct 2014

Exciting times. I'm in rehearsal at the Royal Academy of Music & Claire is working on a scene from Puccini's Turandot for MISSION IMPOSSIBLE V – ROGUE NATION – a Hollywood blockbuster film (!!) (crazy hours hanging around in full wig/make-up/costume & inconveniently a clash with school half-term!)

2nd November 2014

Today Ron rang me at about 10.30am to ask if I could remind him of *his own* telephone number. I assumed he meant his Inglewood number/mobile & rang him back with the details...

But he said *'no, Will, what I want is my father's number'* & mentioned a road in London & it later transpired he meant the house he lived in when he was young near Clissold Park... & said he wanted to get hold *of his Dad...*

I'm afraid I again had to gently disabuse Ron of the idea that his parents are still alive - that since he's 84, they are, regrettably, sure to have passed away. He seemed stunned that he hadn't realised & cursed his memory for again playing tricks on him. I always try to break it to him gently - but it is heart-rending that he genuinely seems to be requesting his Dad's telephone number, really believing he's alive...

I asked him if he wanted your number - or your brothers' – Andrew or Alexander - could he mean the contact details for one of his sons? - but no - he was insistent that he wanted *his father's* telephone number *at home....*

In the end he realised his mistake & I gave him your number again & reminded him that in his kitchen there's a notice-board for useful telephone numbers etc...

Ron did ask me what year his father had died. Do you know the answer? Perhaps if I was able to write down some notable dates in a timeline, this might help him to remember that his parents are no longer with us... just a thought...

In the afternoon today, after we'd been swimming *en famille* in Newbury, we went to see Ron (Claire came too) to check he was alright & to see if he needed anything/any errands. He was again charming & quite enchanting with the children & Claire & very interested to hear that she'd been singing in a concert at the Royal Albert Hall last night.. He does really light up in conversation & is particularly sweet with Thomas & Louisa & seems to really enjoy their company...

16th Nov 2014

On **Thursday** Ron rang at 9.30am asking if I could come and fix his trouser belt which has become tangled. Unfortunately I was about to start a dress rehearsal in Marylebone & unable to help.

On **Friday** Ron rang in a grumpy mood to say that he needed me to take the Audi to a shop & *fill the damn thing up* with lavatory paper - so that he wasn't scrabbling around in the cold flat *in his undershorts* searching vainly for some. I drove to Tesco to buy 5 x 12-packs of Andrex (and some Weetabix).

When we arrived *(en famille)* about 3pm, Ron very pissed off that he'd turned on the lamp on the desk in his sitting-room
& bulb had blown
& everything had gone haywire
& they'd told him he'd have to wait for handyman Rusty to come back to work on Monday morning to get things sorted out....

I did a little investigation & one of the trip switches in his hall-cupboard had tripped, so I flicked it back & this restored the power to those lost circuits. His new phones had therefore lost power - but are now working again.

I replaced a bulb in that offending lamp (& *apropos* of none of the above) when requested, retuned the radio to Classic FM, his preferred station.

49

I told Ron that his trousers were being repaired & he replied that **fifteen days** to fix a zip sounded most unreasonable & he could *sew himself* a new pair in such a time... I'm not sure how he got the wrong end of stick. They'll be ready in a few days. Heigh-ho.

On my return home: Have just rung Ron again to check his phone is working & he sounds chirpy again.

p.s. On Saturday 22nd November I have to go to Aldeburgh, Suffolk - we are holding a short ceremony to scatter the ashes of my great mentor, the theatre, opera & television director Basil Coleman, who died last year. That Saturday would have been Basil's 97th birthday.

19ᵗʰ Nov 2014

..... just a 'heads up' that Ron is talking about getting me to take him to a television shop to buy a NEW TV (!!!)- *Top Secret & GRAHAM IS NOT TO KNOW....* etc etc....so please don't let on that I always grass him up to you...& thus blow my cover as a double agent...

But I'll let you know if this *"Must get new TV"* becomes another obsession in the next few days... He may forget now the television is working again post-power cut....

21ˢᵗ Nov 2014

On **Tuesday** Louisa and I popped in to see Ron in the morning because we had baked some cupcakes & she wanted to take one to Mr. Clempson.

On **Friday** he called to ask if I could come down & write out, in bold letters, his telephone number so he could give it to people when they asked for it. I went to Inglewood to do this (just gave him the number for incoming calls) & also we went through his address book & stuck stickers over addresses that he no longer needs - so that he gets less confused when trying to find people's addresses. In effect this meant that we have covered over details he no longer uses - Totnes taxis from his South Devon Days etc etc... This should make it clearer....

Ron seems to have forgotten about wanting to buy a new television - now that his is working again - but I will keep you posted if he changes his mind again.... (!!??)

One other thing to flag up is that Ron said he stormed out of the Inglewood restaurant yesterday and says he doesn't want to eat there anymore (I couldn't work out quite why) & would I please make him a list of local pubs he could go to for lunch (!!!???) I'm not sure if this is a storm that will pass...

I helped him to put on the oven to cook one of his quiches for lunch in his apartment today before I had to go to pick up Louisa from playgroup. I'm not sure if he'll forget & end up back in the restaurant later today or tomorrow. I'm off to Aldeburgh tomorrow but back tomorrow late evening if he needs taking out to Sunday lunch. But, as I say, by then he may just have forgotten his objections to eating downstairs... (??!!)

25th Nov 2014

Meant to say - thanks so much for your kind words about that newspaper review – I'll attach a really good one from THE OBSERVER this weekend..

We don't do it for the reviews, of course, but it's helpful to have a quotable one... (Though of course, when they're bad, you do tend to want to kill either yourself or the *bastard critic*....)

29th Nov 2014

On **Monday** largely due to Ron's determination to continue his boycott of the downstairs bistro - I took him to M&S & endeavoured to fill the fridge with things that would be easy to cook his usual quiches - but also some of their 'gastropub' pies.... (25 mins in oven) & some already prepared veg. etc... (He asked me to make a list of possible local pubs/restaurants for lunches... since he was adamant he didn't want to eat downstairs.) Ron rang me at 8.40am and asked me to come down & go shopping with him...

When I arrived, I assumed that he'd already had his visit from the nurse for his injections & on our return she was waiting & hadn't known where he was etc... etc... & gave him a stern talking to... She showed me the medical folder in the kitchen & the sheet to check to see the nurses have been & administered Ron's insulin etc. So I can do this before leaving if he asks me to take him out in the morning. The nurses are usually in about 9.30am at the moment.

On **Tuesday** rang Ron but didn't see him. He told me he'd burnt one of his pies that day for lunch... so I'm not sure what he ate... the fridge still full of food....

On **Wednesday** I thought I'd better make sure Ron went out for lunch to ensure he ate something & took him to a new pub/restaurant called The Woodspeen, which he liked very much. In fact, he liked it so much that he said he didn't want to leave the place to go to the 2.45pm opticians appointment I had booked him at Vision Express in Hungerford, so I had to ring & postpone.

On **Thursday** when I went down at 12.30pm Ron had not eaten & I offered to put a pie in oven for him - he said he could do it himself - but I wasn't sure about this... so out we went to the Red House pub for lunch. At both these pub lunches he ate heartily.

Once back at Inglewood he was confused again & asking *if I could ring his father...* it's always a shame to disabuse him of the notion that his father is still alive.... *"I just wanted to talk to him..."*

On **Friday** Ron rang early in a state of confusion - saying that he had been asked to give a urine sample but didn't know who would pick it up. I went down to Inglewood & one of the home-helps was there had another sample bottle. I said I would take the urine to the GP in Kintbury & duly delivered it there.

On **Saturday** (today) I had a call from the dry-cleaners to say that Ron's black trousers which needed repair & cleaning were ready for collection. I picked them up & ran them down to him with the children. He had a packet of tablets which he was taking for his urinary infection.

I told him to try to rest...

7th December 2014

...On Thursday I was on a Shakespeare Marathon at the Barbican Theatre watching a matinee performance of the RSC's HENRY IVth (part one) & about to return for the evening show (part two) when I got word from my mother that my father had fallen whilst out in London and broken his hip & so dashed to find him at the Royal London Hospital in Whitechapel. He is still languishing there & about to have a hip replacement operation... poor Dad. What are we to do with these fathers of ours, Graham?

On Friday Ron rang at 9am. He said that he'd been to the bistro (!) with Mr. Brading and his daughter the night before. I went to see Ron at 4.35pm & found him chirpy - though reporting that his *'Dad'* was coming to see him tomorrow - (I'm sure he meant you). He also gave the impression that he went down to the bistro for lunch on Friday.

Perhaps *Bistro-Gate* - is behind us?

*****

Whilst writing this I've just had a call from Ron who says that he enjoyed your visit & that he's back eating in the Bistro again - what a relief!

15th December 2014

On **Wednesday** at 3am Ron rang in a state of great confusion apparently he'd been for a midnight wander & the staff had to take him back to his room... He left me a message having fallen asleep in his chair I think - he said it was 7am when it was actually 3am....

A new quirk Ron's started to display is to talk about *'the office'*
& his colleagues at *'the office'*
& to talk about coming *'home'* from *'the office'*
& what time he will need me to pick him up from *'the*

53

office'...

I don't think he's consciously drawing a distinction between the bedroom desk and his living-room desk but there's certainly some memory-trick going on here - a casting-back to the old days he used to travel from office to home...

20th Dec 2014

Ron was worried that his coffee machine wasn't working & that we should ring the manufacturers & get them to send their best engineer out, whatever the cost, to service the machine & bring new coffee supplies.... But he'd not unwrapped the Nespresso Capsules I bought for him from Waitrose some weeks back - so I cleaned the machine & got it working for him again & made a coffee for him that, with the addition of two sweeteners, met with his satisfaction...

I saw one of the Inglewood Staff on my arrival who said that he'd been confused & up very early saying that he had to get to *'the office'* & that he thought there was *an underground tunnel* which would take him from his *"home"* to *"the office"*...

Today **Saturday** Claire has gone to Budapest to sing Handel's MESSIAH with the Kings Consort & is away 2 nights - so I'm busy on childcare detail & wasn't able to go & see Ron but he rang & left a message to say that he'd had a bit of a fall but that Maggie had looked after him & that he was going to bed early...

I'll check in on him in the morning
but plan to go to my mother's for lunch tomorrow
& to visit my father in hospital thereafter....

Merry Christmas!

C IS FOR COMPASSION

MR. C:
Will, I'm taking up more of your own time
than I should be.

ME:
Oh, you mustn't worry about that, Ron. I'm
only ten minutes away, when I'm at home.
And then when I'm away working, it's only
for a few weeks at a time. It's never a
problem to pop in and see how you are.

MR. C:
Well, I know that. That's really kind.

ME:
I'm going to head off now Ron and –

MR. C:
Yeah, you do that – thank you –

ME:
.. and crack on with my haircut and then I
have to go to Brighton to see my play.

MR. C:
Okay –

ME:
But –

MR. C:
Frankly, Will, you've got so much to do..
you've got another life…

2015

18th Jan 2015

To: Graham Clempson
Subject: Driving Mr. C

Dear Graham

On **Friday** Ron suggested going out for lunch & that he'd like to return to The Woodspeen Restaurant - a 15 minute drive from Inglewood & which Ron seems to like a lot. Ron on terrifically good form & really enjoyed his lunch. Head Chef & founder John Campbell (again) made a fuss of him & gave Ron his personal business card & said that next time he'll *personally* cook something special (perhaps 'beef cheeks?') for Ron....

Ron was much taken with this personal touch etc...
& heartily recommending the restaurant to fellow residents at Inglewood on our return...

He seems to have made friends with the tartan-trouser-wearing Hamish & both are worried for poor Mr. Brading who is now weak & in a wheelchair following his recent hospitalisation.... I gave a copy of a Woodspeen business card to Hamish at Ron's request...

p.s. one tiny thing to let you know is that Mr. C. has kindly insisted on lending his wheelchair to his friend Mr. Brading - who is less mobile after his recent hospitalisation... the only problem being that I don't now have a wheelchair in the car when taking Ron out... not a biggie - but thought I'd better let you know.. I think Mr. Brading's daughter plans to find her dad a wheelchair & Ron hasn't needed to use his wheelchair when out with me - but I like having it in the car boot just in case he suddenly needs it...

Yes, the shoulder has been a growing problem of late - he says the pain-killers aren't working...

On **Friday** he asked me to lunch at the Red House (that Marsh Benham Pub/restaurant) - for a change of scene - & he had real trouble getting out of his jacket... etc & getting in & out of the car is proving increasingly difficult...

I always make sure Ron takes my arm when walking...
he's still using his walking stick & disdains use of that four-legged metal 'walker'....

Despite a recent run of chirpy form, Ron was pretty forlorn yesterday - I think the recent decline of his Inglewood friend Mr. Brading has moved him considerably... Ron reported that Mr. Brading was wheeled in to sit with him at lunch downstairs the other day.. but the ailing Mr. B was incapable of much meaningful interaction...

25th Jan 2015

On **Friday** when I rang Ron said he was getting bored by going to the Inglewood bistro every day & would like a change of scene & could I take him on a trip to various other possible restaurants & pubs. I printed up a list & we set off at 10.30am & I took him to the Yew Tree at Highclere & got him sample menu & brochure - Ron said he thought he'd been to this place before... but couldn't remember... The Dew Pond (another local place with a good reputation) was closed for lunch but I'll pick up a menu from them in due course... we then drove to The Crab at Chieveley – well-known for excellent seafood - but found it closed for refurbishment. Next Ron asked me to take him to the old favourite Red House at Marsh Benham where we had lunch together. He ate turbot & said it had too many bones - but ate a hearty meal of three courses & drank two glasses of Taittinger...

Ron seemed a bit forlorn yesterday..
I think Mr. Brading's decline has rattled him & said he didn't want to stay at Inglewood *'among the dead and the dying'*.. but I had the children with me & couldn't stay for a long chat.

57

I'll go & see him without the kids tomorrow when I go to sort out laundry payment & see how he's feeling...

I think Ron's need to get away for a drive & lunch on Friday was a desire to dispel his gloominess... certainly it was a gorgeously frosty-but-sunny winter's day the hedgerows gleaming white... & he seemed to relish this outing... & change of scene etc...

Ron tells me you've moved house (?!) - do hope all well on that score & you are happily settled/settling in..

(Of course this may be a complete fiction & he may be referring to some previous removal - as you know, everything is somewhat *'through a glass darkly'* in discussions with your dear old dad...)

2nd Feb 2015

On **Friday** afternoon I had a call from a very cross Ron saying he'd rung me six times & couldn't get through & *what the hell* was wrong with my phone? - or *his* phone? - or phones in general!

I know there's no problem with my mobile since I'd been receiving other calls that morning & don't really want to give Ron my landline again in case he again gets into confused nocturnal phoning *circa* 3am & wakes the children... I think he was probably mis-dialling..

Anyway - that morning I'd had a message that his spectacles were ready to be collected from Vision Express Hungerford (having been sent back & adjusted) & so I picked them up & took them to Ron later that evening & he seemed to have forgotten his earlier telecommunication-centred *conniption*...

One thing to flag up is that Ron thinks that Sally is <u>so very good</u> as a housekeeper that he should retain her further services for administrative/secretarial help & was saying that he wants me to take him to buy a filing cabinet (!) so that she can sort out his correspondence & is talking about buying her a computer (!!) & setting her up at a desk in the hall of his apartment....

(Just thought you should know before your dear father starts forking out for extensive office equipment.... & attempts a recreation of the 1970s Clempson Properties HQ in his Inglewood hallway...)

6th Feb 2015

Yesterday I took Ian C. to see Ron - (that potential new reserve driver I told you about.)
Ron seemed to like him very much - Ian has a background in the construction industry & used to work for Bovis
& Ron was immediately animated & chatty...
& they seemed to hit it off directly...

I rang Ron later to see whether he approved of having Ian as my understudy & he said he was very happy.

8th Feb 2015

..... I went to see Ron at 10am He had lost his mobile phone & couldn't find it & said he hadn't had it for weeks. Ron thought I was a genius (!) when I simply rang the number & found the phone in the pocket of one of his jackets, hanging in the hall...

... I was in attendance when a lady called June and her student Priscilla from the Memory Clinic came to see Ron.

June asked Ron a long list of questions to test his memory - today's date etc - he thought it was September & that the season was autumn. He could spell the word "*world*" but couldn't spell it backwards. She asked him about his state of mind & if he ever had suicidal thoughts & he said he didn't. She asked him to remember three words & then came back to them after a few minutes to see if he'd retained them. He hadn't.

She asked me to fill out a tick box questionnaire on family's behalf observing Ron's behaviours - things like: does he ever have trouble searching for words?
& then tick-boxes for
a. constantly
b. most days
c. once a week

d. once a month
....that kind of thing...

I wasn't able to comment on questions about his morning ablutions difficulty washing/shaving etc as I don't see him at those times...

Ron seemed to think afterwards that the questions had not been in depth enough. I'm not sure what he'll report to you. But he tolerated the strange slew of enquiries with patience & equanimity.

On **Friday** Ron rang in the early morning confused about a diary entry that seemed to imply that he had to ring you. He was a month out - looking at diary entries for February rather than March - but it took him a while to realise & he repeatedly insisted that someone had been into his room & written things in his diary without his approval & that people shouldn't interfere & it makes him very angry...etc. I offered to go down & try to clarify things - but he insisted he was fine.

*****

In due course it became evident that Ron couldn't live on his own any more and needed a live-in carer. And so, in due course, I helped his family move him to a larger apartment at Inglewood.

*****

29th March 2015

On **Friday** I went down to see Ron in the morning taking some bread that Ian C had told me he needed... & had coffee with Ron & chatted & had a catch up...
& made myself scarce when the injection-nurse arrived...
& picked up an idiosyncratically-spelt shopping list that had been left by Amy the stand-in housekeeper
(I think she's been studying too much Chaucer..)

In the afternoon I returned with the shopping
& met estate agent Tony Noon at reception
& took him to no.15 meet Ron for apartment-viewings...

60

As you suggested, I made sure we took Ron to the smaller of the apartments first & then to the more impressive/larger...

In fact he was having a rather confused day & walking with difficulty & very slowly & very exhaustedly. After struggling to see the first apartment, I thought it best to drive the Audi round to pick him up & take him the very short drive to the other side of reception.

It would have been much easier with a wheelchair & I'm not sure if Ron is finally coming around to the idea that he might need to start to use one...

Ron didn't like either of the apartments & expressed his displeasure in no uncertain terms. I'm not sure if he even properly realised he was just in a different part of the Inglewood building & started to say how the apartments were *entirely unsuitable* for him but might suit a young couple *who were just starting out in life (?!)*....

Tony Noon had another appointment to go to in Newbury
& left us to look at the second apartment
& return the keys to reception...

Ron said the entire exercise had been *a waste of time* etc
& that Mr. Noon was patently a perfectly nice chap, but not the kind of agent he wanted to do business with & certainly not the kind of estate agent he was used to working with in London etc...

He said that what he really needed was to find a period property in the vicinity with some genuinely old character & features & that it was futile for modern buildings to try to affect an authentic feel etc...
& proceeded with a critique of shady modern developers
& the various degrees of chicanery they are wont to employ...

Each time I tried gently to suggest that the idea was to view these apartments as staging-posts where carers could be co-resident... he batted away my suggestions..
'But that's not the point, dear boy!'

61

When we emerged from the second apartment Ron greatly admired the Audi parked outside... but seemed unsure that he was its owner & took a little convincing that it really was A3 OLD...

I stayed & made him tea & we talked in strange *non-sequiturs* & airy circumlocutions: as we must on those days when Ron's memory sets itself adrift from its unsteady moorings...

6th April 2015

... Ron rang in the afternoon and invited me to go down to see him at 7.30pm because there was some dinner at Inglewood he wanted to invite me to. When I got there I realised there *was* a dinner in progress for the Inglewood apartment owners with no guests allowed - so I slunk away & hoped Ron wouldn't remember... the nice restaurant staff said he seemed to be having a pleasant time... & I asked them not to say that I'd been there...

On **Thursday** rang Ron & he said *'Where were you, Will??'* - so he *had* remembered my not declaring myself at that owners-only dinner on Tuesday....
I explained the situation
& he was horrified that I had not been allowed to join him as his guest etc etc..
& *who was responsible??* etc etc... I tried to explain - but Ron obviously thought someone on the staff at Audley Inglewood should have been beheaded etc...

Today, **Bank Holiday Monday** ...found Ron on the terrace where he was happily sunning himself & reading the Financial Times (on the first really sunny day since the clocks went forward).

Ron says that he'd like to go to visit the new apartment with Maggie so that she can have a look at the decor & soft furnishings & decide *'with a woman's touch'* which modifications/purchases need to take place before he takes up residence. (?!)

... there is one slightly delicate matter that I feel I should probably tell you - am slightly worried that Ron/the apartment are smelling a bit of stale wee... not sure if the poor thing's got that bladder infection back again - sorry - not the most charming subject but do feel it's my duty to let you know these things... perhaps I should be trying to say something to one of his nurses...? Please advise..

12th *April 2015*

... We just walked down to Inglewood - daffodils & new lambs everywhere..

Saw Ron in bistro - he's on very good form chuckling away & sweet with my kids as ever - looks well & tanned - obviously been enjoying the sun on the terrace!

17th *April 2015*

Ron seems to like Sally & she's good & very caring - even in little things - not least because she makes sure he's not putting on clothing that is food-stained...

Ron seems reconciled to the idea now of moving to a larger apartment where he can have new live-in carers & was asking me if I knew what the timescale was for moving to this regime. I said I would ask you. (Though he does persist in the misconception that he is buying this interim flat & in old-school-thinking that he needs to fit curtains & get a female to recommend interior design choices *'because it needs a woman's touch'*....)

Ron didn't express a desire to go out anywhere this week - though he has been enjoying the sun on the terrace & looks tanned & healthy for it, despite the challenges of his ongoing muscular weakness...

18th *April 2015*

Graham, I completely understand the situation re. sale of the Audi etc. Please don't worry... Hate to think of you *'agonising'* over anything on my behalf!*

I always understood that helping out Mr. C would be a temporary arrangement and, sad as it may be, as the result of your Dad's ongoing decline: it makes absolute sense, in

63

due course, to say farewell to Ron's car....

When I first met Ron, he was happy to make motoring excursions each week, and would, with his stick, accompany me into shops etc. Of late, his freedoms have inevitably been much more circumscribed.

The deterioration in Ron's health has been sad to watch but I am honoured that, in the past months, you have entrusted me with the privilege of looking out for him, in whichever small ways I could...

Please don't forget that we freelance artists are used to taking on gigs that only last a while!

Truth to tell; wonderful things frequently come along to we mad artistic types, who *live in faith,* in the way that Claire and I do. My involvement with The Clempson Family has proved to be another of those Wonderful Things & full of serendipitous links...

(Not least because you & Emma understand my commitment to working with young actors/singers through your connections with the National Youth Theatre, Emma's theatrical background & the other artistic ventures you support. I was greatly amused to turn up at an NYT show last summer & have the Artistic Director tell me that the one & only Nanette Newman had been asking after me! - small world.)

I understand that you are widely engaged in all sorts of philanthropy & I salute you for it. The Kerley Family have been lucky beneficiaries of some of this generosity, in having the use of Ron's amazing car in the past months, for which we are very grateful. I've always chuckled to find myself pedalling down to Inglewood on my rusty old bike & then taking charge of the leather-seated-limo that is A3 OLD!

The nicest thing, of course, has been getting to know your dear old Dad, who is one-of-a-kind & I have loved hanging out with him. The Audi-sale, of course, won't stop me popping down to Inglewood for coffee & conversation with him.

I'm so pleased that Ron is soon to have the round-the-clock care that he now requires. I am sure it will be a weight off the family's collective mind, to know his needs are being consistently attended to.

For myself: I am supposed to be directing my first feature film (??!!) in June (though I'm not counting my chickens because - movies being movies - the project could fall-through or be postponed at any point) & this work would involve shooting each day for a month & then editing thereafter - so I was preparing to hand over my driving/retail responsibilities to Ian C. for several weeks.
(Ian, by the way, has proved to be a perfect understudy.)

The arrangement between you and I has, since the very beginning, been happily, (to quote your term) *loosey-goosey* – so just keep me posted as to developments re. Audi sale & as per usual I will keep you informed with my customary newsletters...

With the arrival of live-in carers for his father, Graham was thinking it might be time for the sale of the Audi and an end to our arrangement. As you will see from the place you've reached in this book, since Mr. C. was still enjoying A3 OLD so much, Graham kindly decided to retain my services and our story continued!

26th April 2015

Ron decided he wanted to go to The Vineyard Hotel Restaurant - but was most dissatisfied with the rack of lamb & sent it back to have it replaced with a piece of beef....

So later in the day I went down to check up on him & found him in a very grumpy mood & Maggie arrived & learned from her that you were on your way down to see him.

He was very agitated about all the things we'd later talked about - the corridor full of wheelchair/box etc... not being able to get hold of his hairdresser (I later tracked down Alan's number & spoke to him & he was going down on Saturday evening...)...
the trousers he'd bought being disastrously too long-in-the-

leg.. & the chap who sold us the trousers was *'patently a nice guy but a total idiot'*.... the timescale for moving to his new house.. *'what the hell was going on with all that??' etc etc...*

& why the bloody hell is Sally (interim housekeeper) writing in *his* diary that she's away for three days & he didn't *'want people writing in my diary willy-nilly'*.. etc etc

Maggie was also trying to get him to try on some new more comfortable shoes & this too was making him exceedingly agitated...& Maggie of course in a very nervy state & trying to get away (I kept saying *"don't worry - you slip away & I'll look after him..."* - but Maggie feeling obliged to help & making Ron more angry & all-the-while incurring the roaring fiery wrath of Dragon Clempson..

On **Saturday** I had a message at 9.30am from Maggie to check that Alan was coming down to do the haircut. I rang back & spoke to Ron & reassured him that yes, Alan was on his way that evening. He then said he was still in his socks (??) & if I came to see him I'd find he was *'still barmy'* & seemed somewhat subdued after the storms of the previous night...

Today **Sunday** I had a message from Ron to say that he wants me to take him out tomorrow to return the trousers & get them altered again as they are not right. I have tried to ring him back a couple of times but have had no reply & have not had time to go down & see him today. But I shall take him out in the morning, once he's had his injections & return to the clothing store with those ill-fitting (they seem fine to me) trousers....

4th May 2015

Hope all well - met new live-in carer Josie today for first time who seems to be doing well learning the ropes... outgoing housekeeper Sally was there at the same time this morning & I think they are communicating well... Ron certainly seemed chirpy...

First impressions of Josie are that she is a kind & caring, safe pair of hands...

10th May 2015

At the lunch, Ron gave me a long speech about how you (Graham) are going into the Care Business & setting up a company & moving from your current commitments into this world of work (?) & so you'll be new to it & need a lot of advice
& how you need to make sure you float the company on the stock market as soon as possible....
& that Ron will help you all he can....

In other news: Ron told me today that he now has someone who comes to help him shave in the mornings as he finds it hard to stand for long enough..

12th May 2015

Shopping... picked up an extensive list yesterday & gently suggested the idea of phasing Josie in to do the trips to M&S... at which Ron had a bit of a rage about interference with systems that were working perfectly well etc....*heigh ho*... will tread gently... Josie, who's just getting used to things.. looks a bit fearful... bless her...

Bistrogate II: Part of the reason for the extensive shopping list yesterday is that I gather Ron's going through another rebellion against the Inglewood eatery - I'm not sure why - Josie made him a quiche for lunch in the apartment... but he seemed determined to start a new boycott.... A staff member told me he went for his lunch as normal day before - so I'm not quite sure what's upset him.... if a carer is with him all day I suppose it's easy for her to make him lunch & might end up saving you money on £15 main courses at Bistro - but not sure of details...

15th May 2015

As previously reported:
Ron not at all positive about notion that Josie might take over from me on shopping duties...
& raging about pointless changes to a perfectly good system... even suggesting that his *eldest son should face a firing squad*...

67

18th May 2015

Slight fly in ointment is that Pam, his busybody neighbour (whom Ron calls "That Fat Woman") has been trying to invite herself
& her husband to lunch with Ron at Woodspeen Restaurant & their last suggestion was for tomorrow.... but I don't think Ron has much enthusiasm for taking them to lunch or for being press-ganged into so doing.... she jumped on him last time I brought him back from Woodspeen lunch & suggested 19th would work for them etc.

18th May 2015 II

One slightly delicate thing I feel I should report:
Josie drew me aside in the kitchen whilst we were making tea, to whisper something about there being a problem with Ron making her feel uncomfortable by calling her *"darling"*
& apparently saying that he would marry her one day
& she said *'though there's been nothing physical'*.

She said that she'd spoken to your brother Andrew about it at the weekend - so I'm sure you are up to speed on this topic. Sorry to bother you with this, not really my business & don't want to speak out of turn, but have always taken the policy with Ron that it's best to let you know whatever I find out from my observations, so that you are kept informed... Perhaps it's nothing more than a simple case of Filipino Modesty v. English Male Chauvinism... anyway... there you go...

18th May 2015 III
Oh Graham what a headache... I hadn't realised the situation was as bad as that (everyone calls everyone *"darling"* in my working-world...) ... Joking aside, not a pleasant thing to negotiate..

Sorry to hear that the Ron-related "challenges" keep on coming...

23rd May 2015

Tuesday was moving day & you know all about that....!
Ron told me today that he was delighted with the new apartment -
'best I've ever lived in!' he declared... (Congratulations!!)

Friday -
Met junk clearer, Sam, at Inglewood who took the stuff away from the old apartment (though not before busybody Pam next door had moved in on those canvas 'director' chairs)

1st June 2015

On **Tuesday** Josie asked me to get a few things from M&S & to buy some new bath mats for Ron as his old ones were getting rather *scuzzy*. I couldn't find yellow ones as requested - but Josie thought the off-white ones I bought would suit perfectly well in the new apartment. *Pisse-jaune* is, I assume, somewhat *passé* these days for your bath & toilet-pedestal matting-requirements...

On **Thursday/Friday/Saturday** I was off to Auvers-sur-Oise in France to watch Claire sing MESSIAH with the King's Consort & so handed over to Ian Crawford. He subsequently reported that he'd popped in to see Ron at the new apartment, but hadn't needed to drive the Audi
& returned the car key to me on **Saturday** night.

I am still heartbroken to think of the last days of Vincent Van Gogh.
Please God send us a little acclaim & appreciation in our lifetimes.
The poor bastard died thinking he was an utter failure.
(Now, of course, his paintings sell for untold millions...)
The horrid bully boys of Auvers-sur-Oise were so foul to him..
rich kids down from Paris in their country houses...
(I've been reading the most recent VVG biography.)

I'm not saying he wasn't seriously disturbed/mentally unwell... But it turns out Vincent probably didn't shoot himself, but one of those little sh*ts was messing about with a pistol & accidentally shot him. Vincent struggled back to his garret at the *Auberge Ravoux* & told everyone that he'd done it to himself... & died in great agony a couple of days later... Just awful...

Very moving to visit the house of Dr Gachet - the physician who was friends with many artists & who tried to help Vincent. It's now kept as a museum - but with no furniture in the rooms - a little like Anne Frank's House in Amsterdam - (which is moving for obviously very different reasons). I always love visiting places like that, where one is separated from great events by time, but not by place...

That's why I'm a sucker for a Blue Plaque when I'm cycling around London...

7*th* *June 2015*

On **Monday** I took Ron to another eye examination he requested, at Vision Express in Hungerford. What I surmised (from my eavesdropping) was that there seems to be little he can do to ameliorate the ongoing deterioration in his eyesight & that the 2 pairs of glasses they made for him in recent months are the best help spectacles can be expected to give...

Josie later reported that he seemed pretty downhearted at this news... He later reported to me that even his genius doctors at The London Clinic are not able to operate on his sighted eye for fear of rendering him completely blind...

On **Thursday** Ron said that he'd like to go out for lunch to The Woodspeen Restaurant.

At the Woodspeen all the staff made a real fuss of him again John Campbell the overall boss & Peter the Chef coming & saying a personal hello etc the waiting staff & *Maitre d'* enchanting him
& Ron had a lovely time & waxed lyrical about the food & sat chirpily on the sunny terrace after the meal.

Ron conspiratorially patted my hand as I was driving
& said he was now able to reveal to me how very fond he is of Josie & that he's asked her to marry him, though she has, with her customary Filipino modesty, currently declined his

70

magnanimous offer.

He says *his brother* (*sic* - presumably meaning you) was nonplussed by the suggestion of his proposal but that he, Ron, has come to the conclusion that he's of an age where he can do what he jolly-well-likes etc etc...

This week I gather Ron has been to Mr. Brading's for lunch & returned the favour by entertaining Mr. Brading (& his carer) to lunch at no.7. He says poor Mr. Brading is in a very bad way & doesn't do much in the way of volunteering conversation these days. (No more Pinteresque lunchtime conversations in prospect, sadly...) Ron left his champagne stopper at Mr. Brading's place & hence his request for a new one.

I spoke to Ron on the phone yesterday & he told me he wanted to buy some garden furniture – deck-chairs and the like & could we do it on Monday...?
I'm not quite sure why he wants garden furniture, since he doesn't have a garden or more than an inch of balcony... will try to work out what he means tomorrow.

Josie rang me this morning on her mobile & said *'Please could you ring Mr. Clempson'* & (her words were unclear but I think she added) *'before I walk out - he's been trying to get hold of you'* - the import of her message seemed to be that she was at the end of some sort of tether... but I'm not sure of the situation... Oh dear.

(*btw* - Ron made a big thing of trying to kiss Josie goodbye as we left for the optician on Monday & she, most unwillingly, proffered her cheek & raised her eyebrows in my direction....)

When I rang back this morning I spoke to Ron & even if he had been fulminating at Josie moments before, was perfectly polite to me & said that he wanted to go shopping tomorrow but seemed to be back-pedalling on the idea of garden furniture... (??)

Next week I'm in Cromarty (on the Black Isle in Scotland) for meetings about THE LITTLE SWEEP - the Benjamin Britten opera that I'm directing there in August. From 18th

71

to 28th of June I'm doing Shakespeare workshops in Singapore & Ian Crawford is primed & happy to cover for me on the Driving Mr. C-front...

9ᵗʰ June 2015

Ron insisted on going & looking at deck chairs yesterday - so I took him to Homebase/Habitat/Hungerford Garden Centre but, as per your instructions, did my best to scupper prospect of any actual purchase...

10ᵗʰ June 2015

Ah Graham - what a headache for you - I'm so sorry - I have tried to take Ron out in last couple of weeks - not least to give carers a break - I'm sure it's pretty hardcore to actually live with him, even if that is the professional deal.. & clearly the bipolar swings between temper tantrum & *"marry me darling"* must be a constant trial... (But I'm well aware you've had to cope with a parallel paternal turbulence since forever...)

Plus: I think Ron's having another bout of that urine infection too - Josie said as much & there was a certain whiff in the car - slightly conquering the aroma of expensive after-shave - poor man - & this always makes his 'behaviours' extra-challenging...

Let me know how I can help this end... & if, as you are rightly threatening, he's going to end up with a Ukranian ex-weightlifter (male *or* female) as his constant companion...

Ron said he'd looked at *"the figures"* & had a chat with you about reining in his expenditure etc & that he was worried he should be *"drawing in (his) horns"* & that you'd said all was okay
& this led to him making the first mention of sale of Audi - so glad if that's now posited without any resistance on his part..

72

14th June 2015

Ron rang me in Scotland to say there was a problem with his telephones (!)
& that he'd spoken to you about it
& that he'd rung 5 different people but no-one had got back to him...& that he had so much he wanted to be getting one with etc etc...
I sent a message to Ian C. to ask him to go down & check out what was going on..
& Ian sent me a text back saying *'sorted'* - so hopefully he was able to pour oil on troubled waters...

15th June 2015

Sorry to hear about Josie's intended departure... oh dear... what a headache for you... Took Ron out today to M&S & Wine Shop & Thornton's chocolate shop... He didn't mention her going - so, no, I don't think he is aware...

19th June 2015

Hi Graham from Singapore...

Glad to hear that Josie's decided to stay... the plot thickens... it's a roller-coaster ride, isn't it?..
hope it's not driving you (two) (too) nuts..

A short report on this week's minimal duties:

On **Monday** Ron decided that he wanted to go out to the shops for groceries
& treats & presents
& to replenish his champagne supplies
(as he's been giving away most of his most recently purchased bottles)

On **Wednesday** I had a call from Ron saying that there'd been a power cut at Inglewood (which there had)
& could I come down & help sort it all out
& that he really was going to have to sell the apartment
and move out if the place continues to be so bloody hopeless etc...

& so I went down to see him & his other carer Jocelyn - the power had been off since
about 2pm & when I got there at about 3.30pm. Jane at Reception said it might be another 40mins to an hour before restoration. Lights pinged on again after about 35 mins & Ron immediately thought it was because I'd intervened in some way (believe me, I hadn't)... in the meantime we were talking elliptically about restaurant table bookings...

Ron was decidedly confused about how many people he's taking to lunch
& on which days & thought that he was taking 15 people to lunch
& that there were two lunches to be planned....
On Monday he had told me he thought he should definitely withdraw £1000 in cash so that he could take his guests to lunch - but I managed to dissuade him from carrying that much cash around in his wallet... & told him that he could pay for things on his card.

Ron asked me to book a table at the Woodspeen Restaurant (his favourite) on 21st - but there were no tables until 3.30pm on Sunday (it's Father's Day & has been booked up for weeks) - so I ended up finding a last available table at The Red House (that Marsh Benham pub Ron likes) for five people on Sunday at 1.30pm....

I think Ron said that your brother Andy and sister Caroline are coming down - but this was unclear... our conversation went round and round the days and dates in that tragic way... as soon as I'd confirmed that it was Sunday, Ron would say Thursday etc etc...

I made two longer-distance personal journeys - one to Heathrow on Tuesday (where I left the car while I flew up to my Uncle's funeral in Edinburgh)and one to Bath to see my dentist for emergency dental work (argh!) before flying 13 hours to Singapore...

Ian C. has taken over on Audi duties until I'm back on 29th.

5th July 2015

Back from Singapore on **Monday**.

On **Wednesday** Ron asked me to take him out to lunch at The Woodspeen which he always greatly enjoys. Paid using Ron's visa card & he asked me to leave extra £10 cash for waitress he'd taken a shine to...

Sad to report that whilst at the restaurant, Ron wet himself before he could get to the lavatory. I didn't say anything about it but found him trying to dry his soaked trousers in the toilet. Poor Ron. Took him home & rang Jocelyn to come down & get him at ground floor entrance....

On **Friday I** went down in the morning to take back the wheelchair from car boot - which I'd forgotten to return to the apartment (after being distracted by the wet trousers return from lunch...) Spoke to Josie about poor Ron having wet himself & she was aware... not sure if they're taking measures to equip him with incontinence underwear etc... Sorry - indelicate subject - but always think it best to keep you posted with health deterioration/developments...

6th July 2015

Taking Ron out this afternoon to buy new shirts at Camp Hopson Menswear Dept. - they know him there & are kind & deploy their tape-measures with patience & good humour - old-style department-store-courtesy, which Ron seems to relish....

Josie declined to accompany us. (I think she cherishes any occasional moments of liberation from the alternating vicissitudes & kissy-kissiness of *Ronsworld*...)

Re. The Two Js & further threatened walk-outs - fingers crossed!

12th July 2015

...Ron was again full of entrepreneurial delusions, riffing on about the inroads you are making in your transition from your current business interests to working in the much

more *dicey-but-profitable* care sector.... (?!)
& how he was advising you in your progress into uncharted commercial waters....
& hopefully that flotation on the stock market is just around the corner etc etc...

Ron's very angry that Jocelyn's husband, John, has been fired (not sure if this is true) & has been advising John that he should take Inglewood to court, forthwith... & that he's thinking of suing them himself (the rotten crooks) on various pretexts... all this, once he's consulted his *father* (which usually means you, Graham...)

Josie asked me to buy yet more new underpants (briefs for daytime use this time rather than nocturnal boxer shorts - went to M&S) Felt slightly weird to be wandering around with a pair of elderly gentlemen's undies in my shopping bag (took them in to Newbury as an example of the kind I was tasked with seeking...)

Later, Josie drew me nervously aside & said that Ron was pretty angry about the prospect of her having 4 days off....earlier, a forgetful-but-fulminating Ron told me the whole system was totally unacceptable... & that he was going to have to change it etc etc....

15*th* August 2015

Just a quickie to let you know that I am back home from directing Britten's LITTLE SWEEP in Cromarty, Scotland.

Went down to see Ron yesterday & did some shopping for him- he seems on pretty good form - though apparently he'd found a load of old files relating to his divorce settlement from Maggie & had sat up late reading them & getting retrospectively stressed about it all - not sure how he came across them...

17*th* August 2015

Over the weekend, I have had several eccentric conversations with Ron on the phone - he's pretty confused - but most benevolent... Josie says he was getting very agitated - insisting that since she is soon to be off on holiday he should be doing the gentlemanly thing & *carrying her suitcase down the stairs...*

Ron also says that he is intending to start legal proceedings against the doctor in Kintbury (for some undisclosed misdemeanour)...

30ᵗʰ *August 2015*

Got back from Nice on **Tuesday**. Despite telling him my date of return, Ron had rung a couple of times while I was away so I texted Ian Crawford from holiday to check in on him & Ron told him it was *absolute rot* & that he hadn't rung me - *'it must have been one of the girls!'*

On **Wednesday** Ron asked me to take him to the Woodspeen Restaurant for lunch. He enjoyed it greatly - the Veronese *Maitre 'd*, Alessandro, making a great fuss of him... & Ron was able to keep me up to speed with the latest of his conspiracy theories on various topics... He says that, against his better judgement, he's decided *not* to sue the GP practice in Kintbury (I've never been sure of the nature of their heinous crimes...)

(re. those cash withdrawals from Ron's card - Josie has been documenting these cash withdrawals too & writing them in a notebook - I told her that I communicate in my newsletters to you about any money Ron has asked me to get for him.. She is scrupulously honest - number two of ten Catholic children growing up in rural Philippines by the ocean - 6 hours from Manila - where her overbearing father wouldn't let his daughters learn to swim - & therefore with a rock-solid conscience/guilt-fixation...)

On **Friday** morning at 08.45 a call from Ron saying that he wished me to take him to Henley-on-Thames for a pub lunch & wanted to take Josie with him.

I went down to pick them up at about 11.30am. But Ron really couldn't remember the name of a particular pub/restaurant & said we should just drive up there & find a place in the high street... & so we set off....

The M4 was screwed Eastbound... My Satnav advised me to

take a detour through Reading & Caversham to get to Henley... but it was the Friday of the start of the Reading Festival - so the town was rammed full of traffic & young people in short trousers & wellies off to get deafened/drunk/high/smelly & dance their t*ts off to their ephemeral idols...

We finally got to Henley about 1.15pm & Ron of course ended up having no idea where we should go for lunch... so I chanced upon The Boathouse (I'd looked it up earlier as a contingency measure) - a good reputation for fine-dining on the river - but a bit *up-itself* in a self-satisfied *nouvelle-cuisiney* way... but I thought it might be okay for Ron who likes the finer things of life & by then I was worried about finding somewhere else acceptable in busy Henley that might have a table for three *pronto*...

Josie sat next to Ron, constantly recoiling from his over-friendly, tactile communication, somehow I did my best to keep the conversation going. I'm sure she'd much rather have stayed at home & enjoyed a few Ron-free hours, as she does when I take him out to the Woodspeen.

Ron became a bit melancholy, saying it was always a mistake to go back to places you'd known in the past. But the mood passed and we were soon laughing at the absurdity of life & Ron's *non-sequiturs* by the time the poncy-puddings came.

"I'M CRUNCHING ON GRANITE" - Ron exclaimed, every time a new dish came with granola or chicory beans or anything with added texture that the pretentious chefs evidently thought might challenge the discerning palate...
& so we scraped aside anything that might further offend his poor old gnashers & left him with the *mousse* or the *jus* or the *parfait* & the softer-parts of the fayre...

The traffic on the way back was APPALLING... sitting in various jams... found our way to the M4 but there had been a serious accident - emergency vehicles shooting past us on the hard-shoulder...

... eventually we crawled past a burned out skeleton of a car - all rubberneckers feeling regretful for our collective

78

impatience & hoping that the poor passengers had got out of the wreck alive & unhurt & *before* it burst into flames...

& then stop-start thereafter - with the inevitable congestion that comes from trying to get west on the M4 Bank Holiday Friday afternoon...

Eventually back to Inglewood about 6.30pm....poor Ron regretful about what a dreadful idea of his it had been to think of returning to Henley at all... insisted I took away one of his bottles of champagne as a sop to my chagrin...

8th Sept 2015

So pleased that Lily is happily settling in in New York. The Hamptons sound wonderful - I've never been either there (or in a helicopter!) or, I should say, *not yet!* Louisa (4) has now started at primary school, *tempus* really does *fugit,* Claire was off in Bucharest singing Purcell, Britten & Handel with The Kings Consort for three nights & relishing the 5* hotel, *jacuzzi*, room service & the peace - whilst I was on Daddy Day Care!

But technology these days is so good - the kids were sleeping peacefully upstairs at home & I was at my laptop & able to see the live broadcast of Claire's concert on Romanian TV - despite being 1600 miles away from the concert hall..

... In the Inglewood Gardens - that purple partition is down so you can see the JCBs, a hundred yards away from the bistro, going about their excavations as the new extension block is constructed... the view over the building site is a curious contrast, scaffolding & machinery - to the terrace view of the sedate crumblies, wobbly knives in hand, digging into their clotted-cream teas....

14th Sept 2015

On **Monday** I went down to see Ron & had tea in on the terrace & Ron told me about watching the racy new BBC serialisation of LADY CHATTERLEY'S LOVER with Josie.... given its subject matter... well... (!?) say no more...

Ron did say he found the screen rather too dark... (?)

Health-wise: Yes, I *have* noticed that his hands are shakier, but generally speaking Ron's been in excellent spirits of late & actually his legs are way better (getting in and out of the car) & I think that's down to the fact that Josie gives him regular leg massages.....

In latest *Grappling News:*
He still tries to kiss Josie on departure, of course...

R: Come here, Josie, darling... give me a kiss...

J: [recoiling - but eventually proffering an unwilling cheek] *Oh, Mr. C, is that really necessary?*

****

This week I took three longer -distance personal trips in the car - chiefly research for my film (which is set around Christmas 1966 about the escape from Dartmoor Prison of Frank Mitchell - an associate of the Kray Twins... they hole him up in a flat in East Ham & then end up shooting him to death in the back of a van - he thinks he is being taken to spend Christmas with Ron Kray at a farm in Kent... I directed a play on the same theme in 1997 with a young unknown actor friend of mine called Martin Freeman - who has now become quite famous through THE OFFICE & SHERLOCK & THE HOBBIT etc... Martin was keen to see the screenplay - & is reading it now - but I'm not sure if he's going to be able to do my small-budget film version...)

So on **Tuesday** I used the car to visit 206a Barking Road (88 miles from Kintbury) - the actual flat where Frank Mitchell was hidden for those 10 days in '66 - a nice Sri Lankan family live there now
& a sweet man called Fareed gave me Tamil sweetmeats
& let me take photographs of his home.... fascinating - of course the interior of the flat is all changed - but the shape of the rooms is the same & the communal stairs/original 1950s features to the block are unchanged in many respects... & then I drove into town (incurring congestion charge) to a meeting at the National Theatre with Kant Pan - a potential editor for my film (his credits include THE CRYING GAME etc - he's very experienced & might be the

ideal foil to my lack of experience as a first-time film director...)

Then on **Thursday** I drove A3 OLD down to Dartmoor Prison Museum (167 miles) to research Frank Mitchell's escape & the Tors on which he was part of a working party..... & take photos... the escape was a very easy affair - Frank just wandered away from a working party, met some of the Kray Gang in a Humber Car & off they zoomed up to London before the alarm had even been raised...

****

Stop Press:
Just had a call from Ron asking me to get him some more cash *'ten or twelve quid will do' (?!)*
& there's a shopping list from Josie, apparently.

Tomorrow - another read through of the screenplay & casting meetings etc & location hunting in Ealing - most of the film's action takes place in a London flat - with a prologue & epilogue with Frank feeding a wild pony on Dartmoor.... though we'll probably have to shoot that somewhere cheaper though Dartmoor is so particular in its look & I'd love to use a drone - cheap new way to get the kind of shots you'd formerly have only been able to do with a helicopter!

All go - scary & exciting....

20ᵗʰ Sept 2015

When I delivered the shopping, Josie emerged looking bleary from another room. I thought she'd been asleep but it turns out she'd been crying because Mr. C had been shouting at her again & said that sometimes she just couldn't take it etc etc... I asked her if there was anything I could do to help - though to me, as ever, he was perfectly sweet & politeness personified... poor Josie, of course, in her resident status, does receive the worst of Ron's wrath.....

On **Wednesday** in torrential rain (which persisted all afternoon - much deployment of oversize umbrella from car to home & hospital thresholds) I picked up Ron & Josie at 2.15pm to take him to the Dunedin Hospital in Reading, as it turned out, for an ECG & then a consultation with a Dr Swinburne & then waited for ages for someone to come & take blood for a blood test.

Had wheelchair to negotiate the warren of corridors & various departments. Much hanging around & then stuck in rush-hour traffic out of Reading. Didn't get Ron home till 6.15pm. Ron railing all the while about how incompetent were the doctors, what a dump was the hospital - nothing like the professionalism he was formerly accustomed to in Harley Street & Devonshire Place at the unimpeachable London Hospital & what was the Kintbury Quack thinking of in referring him for these tests anyway??... etc etc..

I was not party to the conclusions of the consultation - (I'm sure you will have had family-feedback through other channels)- though from my chauffeur's perch, I overheard Josie telling Ron that, yes, as suspected he has some sort of heart murmur & yes it's normal for a man of his age - in short she seemed to be reassuring him that all was well & Ron the while protesting that it was all a pointless waste of time... *comme d'habitude*...

On **Friday** we had a much jollier time - Ron had decided he'd like to have lunch at his beloved Woodspeen Restaurant & again the virtual Red Carpet was rolled out - John Campbell (founder/owner/chef) himself came to chat with Ron & Peter the head chef came to offer him a special grouse dish (which we had as a surprise inter-course-course last week) was available as a main....so Ron had a wood pigeon tart then the aforementioned grouse & then a locally foraged raspberry & blackberry pavlova pudding & Ron raved about each course: *"there are no words to describe the tremendous element of the scenario of my taste buds..."*

In short, he's devoted to the place & they celebrate his loyalty with attention & special treats... My wife tells me the place has just achieved a Michelin star - so John Campbell and his team will be happy bunnies... Must tell Ron when I ring him tomorrow...

I had a sad message from Josie before I picked Ron up -

lachrymose once more - though for a different reason to Monday's tearfulness - her brother had just died - very grateful that I was taking Ron out - locked herself in the loo on his departure so she didn't have to say goodbye in person & could disguise her distress (& chiefly because she was presumably feeling even-less-than-usual like receiving one of Ron's obligatory farewell kisses...)

27ᵗʰ Sept 2015

On **Monday** I went down to investigate Ron's Nespresso machine - which he's been grumbling about & saying isn't working properly
& we should get an engineer out to inspect it etc...
& that he wanted some of the real, delivered Nespresso coffee, rather than the bootleg capsules I've been buying him from M&S....

Lunch at the Harrow in Great Bedwyn, which liked very much, I'm pleased to report: though, sorry to say, he had a bit of an incident - urgently needing the lavatory - just as we were finishing our main courses & I'm afraid poor Ron wet his trousers & asked if I could take him home... which of course I did, forthwith. I rang ahead & Jocelyn was waiting to meet him downstairs & took care of him...

I'm not sure what provision needs to be made for such unhappy episodes of incontinence - as reported previously: it happened once before when we were out at the Woodspeen Restaurant. I'm afraid I don't know what measures can be taken - special incontinence under-clothing etc?... beyond my expertise... All I can do is look after him as best as I can in the case of such misfortunes & get him swiftly home & into the custody of his carers....

Poor Ron.... this is a sad new phase... indelicate, but best that I keep you informed... A shame - as he was on good form & perfectly chirpy until this happened...

Your brother Andrew sent me an email yesterday, saying he was going to visit your father today & asked me to advise him of the secret PIN for Ron's debit card, which I did, via text message, in as artfully obscure a way as I could muster.

The four-digit-number is actually a calendar year a little over 700 years from now, so I made a decoy reference to science-fiction, to disguise the transmission of the magic number to your bro.

Just call me *Bletchley Park Kerley...*

2ⁿᵈ Oct 2015

.... A nice lunch with your dad - he's on good form.
(On the continence front: Didn't pee himself before reaching the restaurant toilet - but, sorry to say, did emerge from gents' toilet with wet trousers...)

He wants to go to Shalborne Classic Car show on Sunday - will try & make this possible...

5ᵗʰ Oct 2015

On **Saturday** morning Ron rang in a rage saying *where was I?* & that he was expecting me etc etc - he thought we were going out that morning & I was *nowhere to be seen* etc...

(We'd actually talked about my taking him to the Shalbourne Classic Car show the following day. Inglewood had included it in their monthly newsletter of local happenings & he'd been keen to go.)

Rather annoyingly, Nida had told Ron you were proposing to visit that morning, so he was agitated when he realised I'd known you were coming & told '*ONE OF MY USELESS STAFF - I'M GOING TO FIRE THE LOT OF THEM ETC*' & that I'd not told him directly - but actually I'd told Jocelyn the night before, because I wanted to make sure your envelope was left in a place where Ron wouldn't find it & be confused by it.

Jocelyn said she wouldn't tell Ron you were coming '*because once, when he heard that Andrew was coming to visit, he didn't sleep at all the night before*'. So, I'd hoped that Nida wouldn't let the cat out of the bag about your arrival. Heigh Ho. I gather he'd been shouting at Nida all that morning.

Ron gradually calmed down on the phone - going round & round the houses as per usual, trying to explain to him that I would be taking him to the Classic Car Show the following day.... *Sunday*, not *Saturday* etc etc & that *'today is Saturday, Ron...'*

On **Sunday** I collected (a much more good-tempered) Ron & drove him to Shalbourne - a Classic Car gathering in a sports field in a picturesque local village - bouncy castles, candy floss, tea & beer tents, brass-band etc... & pushed him around in the wheelchair, looking at the various shiny automobiles antique & modern - he had a lovely time - chatting to some of the car enthusiasts - tea & sponge cake in the marquee etc etc...

(I was a bit worried because there were only *Portaloos* - but no incontinence issues that day, thankfully.)

6th Oct 2015

....The contractors' vehicles in question are a hydraulic crane of some kind used to get to the apartment windows from outside for some kind of maintenance- window painting? - not sure & when they are *in situ* they do block to drive so I can't get the car as close as usual to Ron's entrance as usual - but only a matter of a couple of metres difference... They seem to come & go - the main bother being that the engine/generator is pretty loud as the lift goes up & down....

I'm not sure it really merits a complaint because I don't know how else they'd get access to high windows without blocking the front drive. Also they come & go & haven't been there every day for weeks on end....

Ron, of course, thinks they're a bunch of *layabouts*, forever starting late & knocking off early & making every task last way longer than necessary - (his usual conspiracy-theory-addiction persisting...) Please do be careful out there, Graham... They're all out to get us!!!

19th Oct 2015

Ron wanted me to take him into Newbury on **Wednesday** to look at Christmas Card selections (!) - but when I rang that morning he had changed his mind, partly because Josie was feeling unwell & that was on his mind. He is, of course, delighted to have Josie back in domestic harness (& is particularly sniffy about, by comparison with the saintly Josie, the alleged inferior standards of his other helpers...)

23rd Oct 2015

.... took a sample of Ron's pee down to Kintbury GP surgery. Poor thing seems to have another urinary infection & this is affecting his mind again - setting off his rages with the quaking Josie & Nida that morning...

... up to town to meet an actor called Tom Hughes* (best known for CEMETERY JUNCTION) for a part in my film & then watched him in a play called TICKING with Niamh Cusack at the Trafalgar Studios.. I have offered him a part in the film & his agent is reading the screenplay over the weekend. An actress called Christine Bottomley (whom I met last week & liked a lot) has agreed to play the female lead - very good news.

***Neither Tom Hughes nor Christine Bottomley finally chose to accept the offers. The actors who starred in my feature film THE KRAYS - MAD AXEMAN were the unsurpassably excellent trio of Dairmaid Murtagh, Morgan Watkins and Elen Rhys.**

1st Nov 2015

Ron has decided that he adores the *Ayala* champagne they serve at the Woodspeen Restaurant& asked me to ring Barnaby (at the Naked Grape in Hungerford) & find out more about the product (apparently it's very dry & comes from the same stable as Bollinger) & ascertain a price etc. It turns out it's only a couple of quid more expensive than his current champagne - so he wants me to get him a few bottles... Ron very much likes popping in to see Barnaby when we pick up wine there... & Barnaby always makes a fuss of him (well, he's a very good customer!)

I made 3 longer-distance personal journeys - one with the children for a half-term outing to see Jane Austen's grave at

Winchester Cathedral (30 miles from Kintbury - a village Jane Austen & her family knew exceptionally well) one to Wimbledon (69 miles) & one to Twickenham (66 miles) - both to look at possible film locations.... & tied in a trip to my parents' house...

......This evening Ron rang to tell me that he'd been reading his *Financial Times* & could I explain the recent news-story of the Talk Talk accounts & the hacker who's been able to discover people's personal details etc...? So we had a good talk on the subject of internet security
& passwords & mobile phone contracts that lock you in for 18 months etc & he seemed really quite on the ball about it all & interested to learn about hacking
& modern-day internet security dilemmas....
Some days he can be remarkably enquiring & perspicacious & other days, well... sadly at the mercy of all kinds of volatile delusions....

Ron says that Nida is coming to take over from Jocelyn tomorrow because Josie is still unwell. (Of course, he doesn't remember their actual names, but the import of his comments is clear.) Ron is irritated that Jocelyn seems vague about the **exact time** Nida is taking over from her.

Ron says he **must know** their **exact schedule** & said he was going to give **'my kids'** a stern talking to –
because the way you & your siblings manage your company **(ClempsonCare?)** is evidently a bit lacking & the poor staff members don't have clearly published rotas to work from.....

& with that complaint he wished me a cheery good night...

Graham, I'm sure it must be turbulent at the top of the professional tree, but I know you just had to yield to your higher calling & heed the *Voice of Ambition*... & of course, in the long run, you won't regret your recent elevation from the lowly world of Private Equity to the glamorous & lucrative world of of hiring staff for care homes...

12th Nov 2015

..... Ron said his family lived at **73 Ollerton Road** (the house Ron grew up in that got bombed in the war) - he's never remembered the address before!

& thanks to the internet/iPhone I was able to show him pictures of Southgate Grammar School at lunch & Bowes Road Primary School & remind him who was the head-teacher at Southgate during his time there etc..

& yes - he's talked before about his work looking after the legal affairs of 'lunatics'
& the day he came in to work one Monday (at the Royal Courts of Justice) to find that an aggrieved *widow-of-a-lunatic* had broken in to the office & set fire to various papers....

I think his chat with Eve* really stoked up the memories - he certainly was full of new facts at our lunch today...

& Is it true that your Mum was sixteen when they got married??

Eve was Ron's first wife, with whom he had three children. The recipient of these emails, Graham - and then the twins, Andrew and Caroline. With his second wife Maggie, Ron had two children, Sarah (who he always called Sarah-Jane) and Alex.

16th Nov 2015

....Ron even remembered arriving back at the Muswell Hill flat to find that Eve said she thought the baby's arrival was imminent & so drove her straight off to the Whittington Hospital (?) (that baby must have been you...!)

Though he did then spoil his memory feats by saying he thought his first child was a girl....

21st Nov 2015

Not a great deal to report in this last week before I head off to shoot my movie (!!)

...I popped in to see Ron but he was feeling a bit weak that morning - lying on the bed in his dressing gown, so I didn't stay long. He sounded much chirpier when I chatted to him on the phone the day before.

I will be shooting the film for the next three weeks until Friday 11th December. Nice Ian Crawford will take over Ron's transportation needs in my stead& A3 OLD is in the Inglewood Car Park the while - where I hope the old codgers don't bash it with their execrable parking...

21st December 2015

Ron said that he wants to completely redesign the heating of his apartment & asked me if I would look into finding a heating engineer/consultant who might be able to advise on a new system that would make the apartment heating more effective & efficient....

I learned from Josie that poor Ron had been up in the night & at 2.20am was swigging champagne from the bottle & peed on the kitchen floor. He had no recollection of this until Josie reminded him in the morning & he told me about it with a tragic embarrassment. Poor man.

I gather from Josie that he's doing plenty of dozing during the daytime & then been wakeful in the middle of the night, expecting his breakfast in the early hours etc... tough times.

In the church yesterday morning I found a discarded Order of Service from a recent Kintbury funeral. It was only then that I realised that Mr. Brading had died. That must have been the funeral to which Ian Crawford took Ron & Maggie whilst I was away filming. Sad news.

Messrs. Brading & Clempson were quite a partnership in the early days of Inglewood, in their clubbish corner of the bistro, sharing arcane anecdotes & talking in absurd *non-sequiturs* like Gieldgud & Richardson in that Pinter play *Nomansland*....

Do hope you have a marvellous Christmas & some decent time off with phones set to *aeroplane mode* & ignoring emails*

(*including this one!)

C IS FOR CONSPIRACY

MR. C:
Did I ring you, Will? At lunchtime?

ME:
Yes, Ron - you rang me -

MR. C:
Okay - that brings us up to date..

ME:
Yeah..

MR. C:
... when I called you, and I thought, *'well, if you're not doing anything, perhaps you wouldn't mind coming over,'* and we can at least have a chat -

ME:
Yeah..

MR. C:
... and I will bore you with this wretched story!'

ME:
Yeah!

MR. C:
... and that's what I've done!

ME:
Yeah..

MR. C:
I think... as far as I can remember - okay?

ME:
What do you think -

MR. C:
What's wrong?

ME:
What do you - ?

MR. C:
Now - sorry - I am saying -
ME:
Yeah - ?
MR. C:
I am *preaching* to you -
ME:
Yeah -
MR. C:
That I think *I am the subject of a plot...*
ME:
Right.
MR. C:
Right - it's stupid, (laughing) *stupid,*
stupid - I don't believe it -
ME:
Yeah -
MR. C:
But I am being - either by the girl - the
names I've mentioned -
ME:
Yes..
MR. C:
Have combined - first of all *The Nidas of
this World* have come into my life - from
nowhere - right?
ME:
Mm...
MR. C:
... and therefore there's been somebody,
somewhere helping my girls to produce this
scene - as it is now... *working..*
ME:
Yeah..
MR. C:
Basically - and that's - I'm sorry, old boy
on your mind - to *bend* your mind with this
stupid story - but it is my feeling...
ME:
Yes..
MR. C:
And that is why I wanted to talk to you -
ME:
Yeah -

                    MR. C:
Because you're the only person I can talk
to, to put these suggestions of half *my mind*
and *half me* to you - at the same time -
                    ME:
Yeah..
                    MR. C:
 … and I just get the feeling *I'm being*
"worked on"..

2016

3ʳᵈ Jan 2016

To: Graham Clempson
Subject: Driving Mr. C

Hi Graham

Happy New Year!

Just got back from 4 nights away in Cornwall & rang Ron to say Happy Birthday
- he sounds pretty chirpy - he'd forgotten it was his birthday
- but then seemed to recall that he'd had various phone calls from family members...

On **Wednesday 30th** Ron rang to say that his youngest son Alexander had been to visit with his girlfriend & that they'd drunk all his champagne (!!) & would I get him some more bottles?

10ᵗʰ Jan 2016

..... Ron gave a long sermon about the crooked management at Inglewood... but then moved on to sunnier topics... skiing & holidays etc... he thinks I should definitely take up skiing even though I'm 50 & have never had the chance to try it...

I took the wheelchair with me as I always do, but Ron was happy to walk from the car into the restaurant with his stick (holding my arm of course...).

I get A3 OLD as close to the door as I can & the kind staff know Ron well & help him to his table whilst I go & properly park... He said he thought the salmon was particularly fine.... good to see him relishing his food & relishing life & company following the advent of his 85th birthday...

17th Jan 2016

I made one longer-distance journey in A3 OLD to Two Bridges on Dartmoor - 166 miles from Kintbury - a recce for the opening (exterior) shots of my film - (of course, happy to pay for this diesel). We are going to be shooting the escape of Frank Mitchell on Friday and Saturday this week. I have been editing the film this week - a very exciting stage & weird to be able to make the actors performances better *after they have gone home!* Plus I LOVE adding music - lots of tracks from 1966 that we probably won't be able to get permission to use – but that give a period flavour to the scenes... all fascinating & new territory for me - huge learning curve...

I go to Hong Kong on Sunday - Ian Crawford is primed to take charge of the car & keys. Running workshops/masterclasses for the International Schools' Theatre Association & back on 2nd February.

25th Jan 2016

I drove one long-distance journey - returning to Dartmoor again this weekend where we were shooting the prison break-out from my movie - that's the shooting completed - thankfully Dartmoor weather was perfect - misty when we needed it to be & bright & beautiful too - ponies & running across the Tors with the prison in the background... all in *the can* now - but editing the Dartmoor material into it is going to be a real pleasure...

8th Feb 2016

Ron very agitated a new conspiracy theory: that somehow his B.T. phone hadn't been supplied by B.T. but that the crooks at Inglewood had provided it & that it was part of a consignment of stolen goods & that Josie somehow was in on the deception.... a sad paranoia brewing... said he was 'horrified' that Josie could betray him in this way.. etc etc...

I tried to reassure him that Josie was a paragon of all kinds of virtues - honesty being one of the foremost & told him that your brother Andrew would be with him in the morning & was sure to allay any of these concerns... but tragic to see Ron work himself up into such a state of distress about such phantom fears....

Josie was pretty tired that day. Later, Ron was sheepish, said he'd been shouting at her & would I buy her a present by way of apology? I gather his sleeping patterns have been pretty erratic.

On **Friday** I took Ron out to lunch to a new (to us) pub restaurant called The White Hart at Fyfield - a half-hour drive over the border into Oxfordshire - pretty village pub in ancient timbered chantry building - has won awards for its food in the Oxfordshire Food Awards 2015 & I thought it might be a suitable place - given that Ron's favourite The Woodspeen, was fully booked up that day.

The only bore was that (despite phoning ahead for reassurance) wheelchair-access was non-existent & I had to get two of the burly waiting staff to lift Ron, in his wheelchair, down the six stone steps at the rear of the building.

The food was very good - Ron seemed to enjoy it & ate heartily - though his indigestion is becoming more & more of a problem - he is seized by post-meal spasmodic hiccoughs/belches which take him by surprise & upset him... I did asked if he was able to take a super-Rennie or somesuch - but he says that these interfere with his intestines... & that nothing can be done...

I shan't take him there again - the access problems being too great. A shame, because it was a pleasant place & the grub was good. I'm sure they'd do even better business if they had a decent wheelchair ramp. So it goes.

Conversationally, despite Ron's veering into negative terrain (that Joceyln is useless & that Josie is a darling who should marry him forthwith & the usual lecture about Inglewood villains) – he was mainly merry.

Indeed, I tried to draw him out on happier topics - his early life in London at 73 Ollerton Road etc - war-time evacuation to Yorkshire & a very friendly family he (& his brother?) stayed with (the village schoolmaster?) & he also came up with some happy memories of the Royalty Ballroom in New Southgate where he used to spend Saturday evenings when he was a teenager.   I'll see if I can find some historic photographs of the place on the internet & print them out for him.

..... Jocelyn says that Ron will sometimes yell at her to *'get back to your own country'* & when she's trying to shave him/brush teeth will sometimes try to spit at her.

So sorry to hear of this delusional aggressive behaviour - Ron is very often so charming & kind & I am fortunate to have rarely seen his bad-temper in action. I will continue to try to help to distract all I can - but am obviously not at the domestic front-line - as are his immediate carers.

16th Feb 2016

Sad to report main conspiracy theory this week is that sometimes other people pretend they are Josie & are actually impostors – hard for Ron because he both believes it & yet know this is a delusion... as with most of the *double-think* he is at the mercy of week-by-week...

26th Feb 2016

Picked Ron up at 11.30 & took him out for lovely long lunch at his favourite Woodspeen Restaurant.   Lately it's been pretty well booked-up (it's just been awarded a Michelin star) but today, John Campbell the owner, Allessandro the Maitre d' & Peter the Head Chef all (independently) made a great fuss of Ron & said that I should get in touch directly if the website booking page says they are full & they'd <u>always</u> find us a table. Good to know, as I've found it booked up for the last few weeks at lunchtimes when it would be most convenient to take Ron.... but he has been a very loyal customer & loves to go there... & they treat him like a celebrity guest...

Conversation at lunch started with the usual conspiracy

theories about Inglewood's crooked management & their circumventing of planning permission & other heinous crimes & then Ron saying he really wants to get back to running a business - that he's going to get back in touch with his former secretary, lawyer & accountant & inform them that he's planning to set up a new company & will need their help in doing so.

'Of course', he says, *'my kids don't want me to return to business, they say I should just take it easy, but I feel I should be getting back to it....'*

I then gently steered him onto older memories again of growing up in New Southgate & 73 Ollerton Road & Bowes Road Primary School (which I find out is still going strong & you can read its OfSted report online!) & we talked of his time at Southgate Grammar (merged into Oakwood Comprehensive in 1967) I had my iPhone with me & so could consult the internet-oracle on the Woodspeen *WiFi* - it turns out that Warren *(Alf Garnett)* Mitchell & Ron *(Fagin from OLIVER!)* Moody were both at Ron's school... (a few years before his time...)

We also talked about the local Cinema in Southgate - it was called The Ritz & he used to go to Saturday morning cinema there as a kid & then later as a teenager... he remembers the organ rising up out of the orchestra pit etc...

I find that if I look things up on the internet as Ron reminisces, I can tell him more facts about the institutions he is recalling - today he remembered that he'd been a Sea Cadet (I found out it was the Southgate & Barnet branch) & Ron also said that he thought he'd been a scout & had won some kind of medal - but I'm not sure if he was confusing this for the proficiency badges awarded for skills with knots etc... he said that they'd sailed boats in the park as Sea Cadets...

He also talked about the fact that people who got too posh for New Southgate would move to Palmers Green & from there - if even more upwardly mobile - to the Hallowed Heights of Enfield...

Ron seems to enjoy remembering new things at my

prompting, as if it assures him that his memory, whilst consistently failing him in his current reality, is able to function & recall some material that he thought had been lost. I try to encourage this positivity - I think it's good for him to resurface things he thought he'd forgotten. So often he is cursing his memory... & this can lead to delusion & result in frustration & misdirected indignation...

Actually, Ron was on very good form today & chirpy & laughing away - way better than he's been for a while - a couple of weeks back, I had to cancel our last lunch date as he was too weak to come out.

We had a little chat about his forthcoming operation but he seemed sanguine about it today & ready to entrust himself to the hands of the doctors... not currently *kvetching* about the incompetent *quacks*...

7th *March 2016*

Yes - so pleased the hospital visit passed successfully you're right about Josie - though I think spending the night in the same room as Ron was pretty tough going & thank *gawd* she could tag-team with Jocelyn... but ONWARD!!

21st *March 2016*

On **Monday** the electricity was down at Inglewood - His Lordship was in high dudgeon etc & Josie feeling the icy blast (of his ire) - so I took a flask of hot water to no.7 so Ron could, at least, have his morning cuppa. Power was, I gather, restored about 10.20am.

Poor Ron was feeling weak that day. Josie asked me if I could go to the Mobility Store in Marlborough & buy a hospital-style table that could be wheeled up to a bed/chair - which I duly did. I also went to Boots to buy pull-up incontinence pants for Ron.

I later had a call from Josie to say could I please get Ron *'the biggest box of chocolates'* from M&S. Apparently he had become very insistent that he needed the largest box of chocolates possible.

....I heard the next day that the box was sufficiently sizeable. Not sure why Ron had become obsessed with choc-box size. Josie later reported that he wasn't that keen to actually *eat* said chocolates but, for some reason, needed to know that the purchased box was a whopper.... so it goes...

Never mind the quality, feel the width...

On **Sunday** Josie rang to say that Ron urgently wanted to speak to me - to clarify arrangements for hospital trip on Wednesday, I think - though his phone call was pretty confusing. He then rang me later on his mobile on two separate occasions & deeply apologetically, said that there must be a fault with the machine that, of its own mechanical volition, repeatedly rang my number.

****

... in the evening my wife and I drove to the Barbican to see a concert performance of George Benjamin's opera WRITTEN ON SKIN - of which I am going to be directing the US premiere - at Opera Philadelphia in February 2018. This is a very important gig for me - directing a first US production of a new opera is a real dream job... I've directed two previous shows at Opera Philadelphia - but this is the first in the huge main-house theatre...

It was lovely to be out on the town with my Claire yesterday - truth to tell, we are at that stage with young kids where childcare is pretty hard-won... so the chance to spend a few hours together - let alone finish a conversation - is realistically rather seldom & a great pleasure to actually see each other outside of the horse-trading/exhaustion/relentlessness of family life... (of course these tiring times are the very ones we will be looking back on & pining for, in 20 years time when these selfsame pesky kids have grown up & flown the nest & have no great desire to hang out with their dull, annoying & aged parents...)

29th March 2016

On **Wednesday** picked up Ron & Josie & Jocelyn at 8.15am & drove to hospital - dropped them off & drove round & round looking for a parking space... sent up a

prayer to the parking gods & one appeared just outside exit... Came to meet you & you know the rest....
Took Ron home - Josie was short of incontinence equipment so quick trip to Marlborough Mobility shop for pads & aprons & gloves..

... to The Woodspeen. This was the first time Ron stayed in his wheelchair through lunch - even at lunch table - but it seemed the best policy... he ate heartily & was on chirpy form... He even remembered a new fact he'd not told me before - in WW2 I knew he'd been evacuated to Yorkshire - but at lunch he remembered the name of the village – he says it's a place called WIBSEY.

I proceeded to look it up for him on my iPhone - it's on the outskirts of Bradford - Ron didn't remember much more than the name - but previously he's told me that he stayed with a schoolmaster & his family... He said he was there with his brother (?) - but, to tell you the truth, I've never been clear on the number of Ron's siblings... did he have brothers & sisters? Very often, in his confusion, he'll tell me that you & Andrew are his brothers etc etc...

We were back at Inglewood around 4pm, Ron seeming tired - but with his spirits lifted by the escape from the Inglewood Compound.

On **Easter Monday** morning I had a call from Ron saying he urgently needed to talk to me - would I like to take him out for lunch today & could I also take him to the optician to check his eyesight/glasses again? I told him that I unfortunately had plans for family walk & picnic & that, it being a Bank Holiday, the optician would be closed.

But we popped down *en famille* & found him having lunch in the Bistro with Maggie & Josie & gave him an Easter Card the kids had written & a small gold-foil-wrapped Lindt chocolate bunny. Ron, not realising that it was made of chocolate, said he would '*have it mounted on his car bonnet...*'

This week I am running workshops for British Youth Opera at South Bank University. They are young singers - most of whom are currently studying at UK conservatoires & I love

100

to help them to improve their acting & encourage them. There are so many toxic bastards out there who spend their whole time telling young artists why they shouldn't have a go & pursue their dreams & I, being of that crazy tribe, am happy to try to encourage them that actually sometimes tenaciously held dreams can come to fruition..

25th April 2016

25th April 2016

On **Monday** had a text message from Jocelyn to say please could I urgently bring champagne by the next morning - because Mr. C. was freaking out that he was down to his last bottle...

As you will be aware, things were a bit tricky all week because Josie away. Plus Jocelyn said she thought Ron had another of his urine infections & that always affects his temperament...

On **Tuesday** I went down to collect a urine sample & deliver to the GP. Ron told me that day that he was considering building some new houses *"4 to 5 bedroom detached places around and about this locality"* and proposed putting them on the market for £60,000 each. He seemed intrigued that property prices in this part of West Berkshire are rather more inflated these days....

When I got Ron back to the apartment he became agitated about there being no carer present & that he wanted to talk to his kids about changing the whole arrangement - firing the team and starting again & insisted that I rang you - which was when you had that text from me asking if you were around...

Sorry to have bothered you - but was looking for some pacifying information. When I said that you were in an important meeting, but would call him back later, Ron calmed down immediately. Jocelyn returned to the apartment about 4pm & took back the care-reins...

On **Saturday** early in the morning Ron rang and asked me to take him to lunch that day. Unfortunately I had other plans: a trip with Thomas (7) & his maternal grandfather (73) to see Aston Villa play at home. Poor Thomas,

The Villa are having a dreadful time & all we can do is reassure him that it's very noble to stick with a team through thick and thin. Grandpa, after all, has been supporting the team since he was a boy & seen many triumphs and disasters along the way.

I tagged along but, knowing little about football, have to confess I find the whole thing a bit scary. A theatre audience may be bitchy, but they certainly aren't adversarial in that savage/sporty-way. The millionaire players bounce around the billiard-table-green-turf like young gazelles, with the occasional fit of babyish histrionics. A strange game. Aston Villa lost 4-2. They will go down to what used to be called the Second Division next season, or so I am given to understand, by the experts in my family.

Ron was much calmer & sweet-tempered in the latter part of the week - again once he is on anti-biotics & the urine infections are at bay - he becomes his kindly self again...

2nd *May 2016*

I got back from Munich last night & seeing the historical sites of the inexorable rise of the Nazis...& developing a piece of theatre with International School students on that dreaded theme...... and, today, on my return to the United Kingdom, Mayday Holiday here was all very *Hitlerjugend* - Louisa (5) & her brainwashed primary school cohort, goose-stepping around the Maypole on the Village Green, the crowning of the scary little Aryan May King & Queen & a truly terrifying platoon of Morris Dancers in Church Square...

And so, in just a day, I made the transition from the German brand of Fascism to Ye Olde English version...

4th *May 2016*

Stop press:
Greetings from International Peacekeeper Kerley...
Currently typing this from my laptop on sofa at Apartment 7...

Had this message from Josie at 8.30 this morning:

Hi Will - Good morning can you please do me a big favour, Mr. Clempson is being difficult and verbally abusive towards me that every time I go to his room to help he will tell me to bagger (sic) off pack my bag and go.
I just want you to be here to make sure I can get him ready for you.
I know he will be a different person when someone is here.
Thanks Will
Josie

So I came down to Inglewood at 9am & found Josie weeping in the kitchen *'He's just so rude - the <u>words</u> he uses'*
& Ron in bed, but full of contrition - *'I think Josie's gone - I sent her away - but that's just the way I am and if she's left then it's my own fault...'*

Josie dried her eyes & went to see him & Ron apologised profusely (& tragically..)

I'll sit tight to make sure there are no further skirmishes & take him to optician at 10.50am & then on to Woodspeen lunch to give Josie a bit of space...

Sorry to bother you with this -
but always best to keep you informed...

Warmest wishes from the sunny battlefields of West Berkshire...

5th May 2016

...I took Ron to Vision Express Hungerford (where he insisted to the optician that he was still *driving a car* (!!) - don't worry - he really isn't!) & thereafter to Woodspeen Restaurant...

The Optician gave Ron thorough examination & happily tested all those spare pairs of specs Ron has been keeping & sent the useless ones off for recycling..

Ron said he thought she was an excellent optician, very thorough, perfectly professional and, in time-honoured Clempsonian fashion added: '... *and she's got a great pair of legs'.*

Josie still saying she wants to leave... I just try to be sympathetic ear... & *lay me down* (*like a Bridge over Troubled Water...*)

16th May 2016

On **Monday** Ron rang early to say that - *mirabile dictu* - he'd fixed his watch & it was amazing.. I later worked out that he'd been examining the perfectly-functioning clock on his mobile phone & got confused...

One of my meetings this week was with my opera agent, who says he no longer wants to represent me. He says, in these tough times of austerity, he is having to halve his roster of artists. I am obviously not making him enough cash. B*ll*cks....

But I feel somewhat sanguine about this rejection. I've got a feeling there are other (perhaps bigger) fish to fry that might just mean I will get better representation. I certainly need to get a film agent now.

We freelance artists live in faith. And, anyway, to tell true, whenever I met him, I always found my opera agent well-meaning, but a bit dull. And he certainly didn't get me any gigs, but still took his 10% (plus VAT) commission (*comme d'habitude*)....

22nd May 2016

Thank you very much for payment for last week & for your kind words about agents/representation... Completely agree - I think an agent has only ever been really instrumental in getting me <u>one</u> job - putting me forward to direct a Richard Bean play at the Bush Theatre - the rest has been me getting my own gigs & then having to pay them a goodly percentage of my fee (plus VAT)..

On **Monday** Ron rang & asked if I was up for taking him to

104

lunch that day... unfortunately I was booked in to my dentist in Bath for much drilling & fitting of another crown on my poor knackered old molars... too much sugar & too many sweets as a kid, methinks... for example: my Mum (bless her) used to give us an orange cut into pieces with a little mound of granulated sugar to one side since *'oranges are so sour'*..- but that generation used to have at least two sugars in every cuppa etc etc...

Another sign of time passing is, sadly, Ron's increasing reliance on the wheelchair. One reason the Woodspeen is such a good venue for Ron is that it has level access, all the way from the car into the restaurant table. Plus, Ron loves it there & they make a real fuss of him - John Campbell the proprietor comes to say hello & lays on an extra *amuse bouche* or inter-course titbit... mind you, I bet we're their most regular clients by now... I always ask Ron if he'd like to go somewhere else - but he seems perfectly happy there...

I took that family tree your brother Andrew created & tried to draw Ron out on the subject of his siblings... but he really wasn't able to dredge anything up & seemed unable to remember having brothers & sisters at all...

He did have another episode on the way of trying to tell me that his Mum & Dad had been to visit him at Inglewood & that they'd had a lovely meal together. Again it was tricky to gently break it to him that his parents have long since gone off to the other Ollerton Road in the Sky...

On **Thursday** in the morning I went down to Inglewood to see Ron & we had a long chat about the EU referendum & Brexit v. Remain & politics in general... He was on good form that morning & we chatted merrily for some time & laughed a lot...

That's why it was sad that day when we returned to Inglewood with shopping, that he wasn't feeling well - I think he was being sick into a bowl with Nida taking care of him he called *'don't come in, Will!'* - because I think he could hear I had the kids with me & he didn't want to frighten them... & so I kept the children out of the way & we made a quick departure without seeing him.

105

Poor Ron. The awful act of vomiting has got to be, for all of us, one of life's most bleak & miserable moments.... I always feel *grim-issimo* whilst '*shouting to Raoul down the big white telephone...*'

.... off in to town for a meeting with Stephen Johns, the Artistic Director at the Royal College of Music. I am trying to get them to put on a centenary concert/event for my friend & mentor the director Basil Coleman, who would have been 100 on 22nd November 2016. In his will, Basil left half of the sale of his house in Barnes to the Aldeburgh Festival & half to the Royal College of Music.

They jolly well should put some effort into hosting a celebration for Basil - since both organisations benefitted to the tune of over a million quid each.... The RCM are now saying they probably can't put something together in time for Basil's birthday & that it'll have to be in the spring...

Basil was the original director of many of Ben Britten's operas & was very kind to me. Long story. I owe him a great deal. He always said he wanted me to get into directing film & TV - so I suspect that when he headed off to the Pearly Gates in 2013 he must have had a word with the powers-that-be & that's led to me being asked to direct my first feature film.. Bonkers..

If you're interested: here's a link to the obituary I wrote for Basil in *The Guardian*

23rd May 2016

Must just tell you that your dad has just rung me - at 4.45pm - sounding on chirpy form but said "*I don't want to stay the night here at Maggie's place, so I'm wondering if you're free to run me up to North London & take me back to Mum & Dad's place in Ollerton Road...*"

It then took a little while to untangle his confusion & to bring him up to speed with his current living arrangements..& the current whereabouts of his parents etc...& that there's probably a different family living at number 73 Ollerton Road... but he took it all in good part & ended up laughing about the tricks his memory is playing on him...

Thanks so much for telling me about that weekend visit from your mother - yes - I was confused when he started talking about a wife in the kitchen & how fantastic it'd been to live with her – didn't know he was referring to Eve in that first flat they had in Muswell Hill...

25th May 2016

Had a nice Woodspeen lunch with your dad yesterday & he was on very good form.. ate heartily & purring the while because the thinks the food/service there is excellent...

Two little "heads up" if you're seeing him tomorrow:

1. Ron is complaining about his bed - he finds it very uncomfortable (haven't examined it in detail but I think the new one is more of a hospital bed now than the normal domestic ones he's had previously) & says he wants me to take him to a bed shop so he can buy a new one... currently stalling on this... I imagine the hospital-type bed means it's much easier for carers to get him in & out of bed & stop him falling out in the night...

2. Ron rang me last night to say that he would like me to find him a trustworthy local agent with whom he can work on selling the various flats he owns in his block at Inglewood (!)... I tried to gently disabuse him of notion that he has vast property portfolio there (he doesn't, does he??) but he really wasn't hearing it... I said I would do some research... (to pacify & distract) I haven't spoken to him yet today so don't know if he's forgotten all about it....

Anyway - just thought it might be useful for you to be aware of these current hobby-horses if you see him tomorrow...

27th May 2016

Writing this on the train home from London meetings with composer/producer about the music for my film.. sometimes the meetings you are most nervous about prove to be the most rewarding - or perhaps that's just the thrill of surviving them...

107

This week, Ron has been a bit confused about where he lives & has asked me on two separate days, to pick him up & *take him home* & said that he didn't know how he got here (Inglewood) & that he needed to go *back home*....

Josie rang to say he was getting in a bit of a state & very confused & thought I was coming - so I went down to Inglewood for a couple of hours in the afternoon & we had tea & chatted & ended up having a thoroughly pleasant time looking through old photo albums - which actually perked him up a treat & I hope distracted him from earlier agitations... nice photos of your mum when young & even the family he was evacuated to in WW2... great stuff & he loved explaining them to me & deciphering the writing...

6ᵗʰ *June 2016*

Greetings from Brighton where I started rehearsal today for a new devised play (working title) ENTER THE DRAGONS - about the ageing process in middle-aged women and the multitudinous crimes of the Patriarchy... (hell yeah!)

....Rang Ron & went to see him on **Saturday** morning for coffee... Nice to see him & he was on pretty good form. My Louisa (5) sent him a postcard from Cornwall & luckily it got to Inglewood before I did. I showed it to him & talked about Fistral Beach - which he has formerly said he's visited - but he couldn't dredge up any memories about where he stayed etc. I showed him a picture of the main hotel there - but this didn't trigger any recollections... though he did have a memory of it being good for surfers - would he have surfed down there in Newquay??

...Ron rang me in Brighton today to ask me about cars - he seems to think that he has other cars parked in various garages & was rather confused about it & had I got the keys? Jocelyn says that she took Ron down to the Inglewood car park the other day to look at A3 OLD - thinking he wanted to see his car - but he said *'no, not that one - my sports cars - I have two...'*

108

14th June 2016

I return home on Thursday night with design meetings in London on Friday about WRITTEN ON SKIN - the opera I am directing for Opera Philadelphia in February 2018. Mine is the first new US production. Scary & exciting to be directing a show on the main stage at Opera Philadelphia & about as good as it gets professionally. My Dad always used to say, in a kindly-but-pitying way that depressed the hell out of me: *'we'll see your name in lights one day, son'.* My psychological baggage means that, like reaching the stash of gold at the end of some accursed rainbow, it never feels like I fully arrive at whatever he must have meant....

My first feature film THE MAD AXEMAN is being submitted to the panels this week for both the London Film Festival & the Toronto Film Festival. Gulp & fingers crossed. If it's rejected & ends up a poorly reviewed turkey & goes straight to the DVD remainder-bin at WH Smith, I'm sure I'll want to go down to the railway line at Kintbury Level Crossing & throw myself onto the rusty tracks.. so it goes.

Now, before rehearsals start at 10am, I must get back to the script of our newly-devised feminist polemical play: **ENTER THE DRAGONS** in which **The Village** is being ravaged by **The Monster** (whom we later find out is the Ageing Process/Menopause) & inspired by **The Mentor** (a many-headed puppet-combination of Jenni Murray from Women's Hour, Germaine Greer, Annie Lennox & Dolly Parton) our **Protagonist** (Everywoman) is sent off on a quest to slay **The Dragon** that is abducting & dispatching our women-of-a-certain-age...

In short: just another day at the office...

2nd July 2016

... at the Woodspeen, Ron was particularly struck by a Romanian waitress called Bianca - & observed & remarked on her various attributes in his unreconstructed 1950s way.

11ᵗʰ July 2016

On **Monday** (4th) had a rather odd message from Ron - when he heard it was my answer-phone he hissed *'Bloody Man!'* & then hung up & then later Josie rang to say that he was agitated
& would I come & calm him as he'd got the impression *I'd pinched his car (!)* –

I went down to see Ron at 5pm - there was much talk of needing his car to go to the office later
& where was his *'real'* car parked - his sports car? - was it in the garage? -
& the usual perennial transport delusions - he is adamant that he can still drive
& *who gave me the impression he couldn't???* etc etc...
but managed to calm him & we ended up having a nice cup of tea & a chat...

At lunch, partly as a memory exercise - I was trying to draw Ron out on the subject of National Service - since he was born in 1931 he'd absolutely fall within the remit for conscripted National Service - (my Dad, who was born in 1934 did two years in the army between '55 & '57). Ron seemed to think he might have been in the Fleet Air Arm - but your sister Sarah Jane later said she thought he may have been exempted on health grounds, citing his blindness in one eye.

(When did Ron lose his sight in that eye? He gave me to understand it was a result of his diabetes.. but did the blindness develop when he was much younger?)

In saying he thought he was in the Fleet Arm & on aircraft carriers (??) perhaps he may have been confusing his teenage time in the New Southgate Sea Scouts with a time of military service. But as so often everything is a bit 'through a glass darkly' with your dear Dad's memory... If anyone has further information - I'd love to know it so I can discuss it with him... these journeys down Memory Lane often really perk him up & encourage him that he isn't losing the plot completely...

18ᵗʰ July 2016

Ron rang me this morning to say that congratulations were in order because Josie had consented to have him move in with her to her apartment at Inglewood... (??)
I went down to pick up a small phial of amber nectar in my capacity as Urine Courier
& took it down to the GP in Kintbury. Had a coffee with Ron - he was suggesting a proper drink - (I think in celebration of his new *'marriage'* to Josie....)   He was asking me the name of *'the other girl - the one who lives downstairs'* (Maggie) and saying that *'she told me I was married to her once, but I'm not so sure....'*
I managed to carefully steer him onto other less turbulent topics....

Josie took me aside & said that he seems to think that they are *'a couple'* & she gets very nervous of disabusing him of the idea, lest it makes Ron angry... etc etc...

On **Wednesday** afternoon, Ron rang to ask if I'd come to see him because he was convinced that his carers were trying to *'work on him'*. Josie was knackered & had gone off for a rest while Nida was in charge.

Nida had told Ron that Josie had gone shopping. She hadn't, in fact, but had just crashed out in the bedroom, having been up all night ministering to the Sleepless Master.... I stayed for a cup of tea & managed to distract him from his various conspiracy theories..... the poor man sometimes seems to think that he's at the centre of a GASLIGHT*-style plot to drive him mad...

On **Thursday** Ron rang at 9.30am to say it's a lovely sunny day & would I take him out for a drive & to lunch (again)?... & so I jumped to it & picked him up & took him on an hour's circuit around the local villages & beauty spots & actually Ron relished the sight of the countryside hereabouts in the bright sunshine...

We went to the Crown and Garter - a traditional pub in Inkpen which is under new management & we sat in the sun in the rather beautiful garden with Ron purring contentedly... As you know, once outside, he always

111

disdains shady tables in favour of direct sunlight - (I'm more of a shade-person so I was glad I remembered my wide-brimmed hat to keep the hot rays from my sad bald pate. Ron, even at 85, has been lucky enough to keep his extensive thatch. Bodes well for you Graham, I shouldn't wonder.)

If you're not familiar with the reference, GASLIGHT is a Patrick Hamilton play turned into an Ingrid Bergman film from the 1940s where a wife is made paranoid & persuaded she is losing her mind by her evil husband who is deviously trying to dispossess her etc etc..

25th July 2016

On **Saturday** went to see Ron & picked up another shopping list from Jocelyn. Chatted with Ron & he said that he wasn't going to be living there long (meaning Inglewood, I think - though his soliloquy was pretty opaque) & that he was going to go back to Ollerton Road and live with his mother – he didn't know if his father was still there as he hadn't seen him for a long time. He wasn't sure if his Mum and he would be able to get on since they both 'had their own ways'...

28th August 2016

....this was the day I again acted as Ron's Chief Urine Courier, or, as my wife rudely calls it, *The P*ss Taker.*

Nida had said that Ron was desperate to go out to lunch & so on **Saturday 27th** I took him to the Woodspeen which he loves. John Campbell (the proprietor) appeared & gave us a couple of fine baguettes, freshly baked that day in his Cookery School across the road from the restaurant. Ron purring all the way through - he finds the food there excellent, thank God - great to have found somewhere that meets with his consistent approval. Ron told John Campbell that he thought Jay Rayner's *Observer* review of the restaurant was a disgrace & indeed actionable & offered his help if John wanted to sue the newspaper for defamation/libel.

In behavioural news:

Ron has been charm itself towards me - but sadly, I gather from Josie that she had to call out an ambulance at 2am one day because he was being so difficult. I didn't get to find out any further details of the incident.

Nida tells me that one day Ron told her to *'f*cking drop dead'* & told her that he could cope perfectly well and what the hell was she doing here anyway? Why didn't she just *p*ss off home?* She told him that she had to stay, that it was her duty to be with him through the night and he said *'well, you won't be getting paid'* & was full of venom & then of course, some hours later, when he needed practical assistance, said *'thank God you're still here'* & was remorseful & regretful....

I think it doesn't help that (in his thoroughly un-PC & unreconstructed way) he finds Nida singularly unattractive & reckons himself effectively married to Josie, so finds Josie's absence particularly aggravating.

7th Sep 2016

.....sending you all best wishes from Oscar Wilde's cell at Reading Gaol – long story – but there's a very moving exhibition here currently...

12th Sep 2016

Chatted with Ron on **Monday** & he said he'd like to go out to lunch the following day. Nida reported that he had her up at midnight saying that he needed to get ready to go to lunch with Will. *Oh, dear.*

On **Tuesday** I duly took Ron to his beloved Woodspeen where he ate heartily. Having returned him to Inglewood, I went into reception for a leak in those nice decadent bogs (with linen flannels for hand-towels) & there was Maggie in the library who beckoned to me.... She asked me how I was finding Ron in terms of the deterioration of his memory/mind etc....

I then took that opportunity to find out from her a little more about his family & learned the extent of alienation from Ron's parents that happened at his break up from your

113

mum & about (gay) brother Paul becoming his parents'
carers.... About Ron's antipathy to homosexuality (which
he's never displayed in my hearing). I hadn't realised the
extent of the estrangement - so curious that Ron now talks
so much of going to see his parents & staying with them &
moving his furniture back to 73 Ollerton Road etc...

Maggie also talked about their marriage & your father's
inability to apologise - how strange it is now that he's
frequently so very apologetic... something in his character is
gone & something regained in his puzzled dotage... That she
hadn't wanted to move to the oversize Soundess House - but
that Ron has always been status-driven etc... etc...

It was good to talk to Maggie actually, because, despite your
brother Andrew supplying that invaluable family tree, I do
get so confused working out Ron's biography from the
current flux state of his memory - not least because he
confuses sons with fathers & indeed his whole grasp of
familial nomenclature is in a murky disarray. Poor Ron.

Jocelyn drew me conspiratorially into the kitchen & gave a
half-hour speech about the problems between her & Josie &
Nida.... again, like a weedy vicar I nod & make sympathetic
faces & say *'O dear, O dear..'* and try to be kind in my
ineffectual way, in the meantime thinking that I'm going to
be in deep water with Mrs K if I don't get home in time to
dunk the children in the bath & read Louisa's bedtime
story... so it goes... *always in trouble, only the depth that
varies....*

I made one longer-distance personal journey - to
Ravenscourt Park tube to leave the car when I went into
town on Friday to see OWEN WINGRAVE the opera
Benjamin Britten wrote in 1970 for television broadcast.
Most people think it's his worst opera. But I don't think it's
found its time yet. British Youth Opera were presenting it at
the Peacock Theatre. I've directed 5 shows for them at the
same venue & it was nice to be in the audience without
having to worry about anyone falling off the stage on my
watch... i.e. as punter rather than director.

19th September 2016

On **Wednesday** Josie said that Mr. Clempson was very lonely & had been asking if I'd take him out again... we went for a sunny drive in the local countryside which he much enjoyed - there's an old windmill at Wilton... & pretty villages hereabouts that he likes to see & ended up in the bright sunshine on the last day of the Indian Summer at the Crown and Garter - that pub in Inkpen with a pretty garden that Ron was previously much enamoured of...

When we got to the pub, Ron suddenly looked somewhat distressed & started pointing at his mouth - I couldn't tell what he wanted & he proceeded to vomit down the side of the wheelchair & onto the pub garden patio.

I grabbed an industrial-sized roll of blue kitchen-tissues from the kindly bar staff & I cleaned it up directly - none had actually gone on Ron. He kept retching for a little while.. I made multiple offers to take him straight home to his carer - but he was insistent that he wanted to stay the pub. He quickly brightened up & we had a light lunch - he ate a small piece of fish & some strawberries & ice cream & said he had no idea where the sickness had come from.

I reported this health incident to Nida on our return to Inglewood.

On **Thursday** Ron had a very confused day. He rang in the morning - still in one of those delusional dream-states that often strike him early in the day, when he seems to have been fathoms down in his sleep-world.

Where you or I might instantly shake off the content of a dream within the opening few seconds of our return to the quotidian; Ron sometimes seems caught in a netherworld, where there is tragically no True North...

In the afternoon I rang again & Josie said that she was making herself scarce as Ron had been shouting at her and threatening to '*chop her head off*' if she came near him...

I went down at 6.45pm & found Ron getting into bed saying that he'd fired Josie

115

& that it was for the best - *'she's not happy, I'm not happy'* and that he was sure that Josie had left for good (she was actually in the next room, of course & waiting for peace to break out).

He rather plaintively asked me if I could help him to find a psychiatrist who would be able to help him. I spoke to him about trying to let go of having to be in charge of things, of trusting that all his family, carers and friends wanted the best for him etc etc...

There was huge storm brewing that evening & then flashes of lightning & thunder & torrential rain - which gave Ron's tragic ravings even more of a sense of King Lear - impotent and divested of his kingdom, but still raging for control and pleading for his sanity.... we had the bedroom balcony door open & from the height of his window, at the level of the trees - there was even more of a theatricality to the occasion...

O, the pity of poor lost King Ron...

He was much calmer when I left him that night.

The storm had subsided.

That evening, Ron rang asking me how he was going to get back to his parents' place in Southgate *'where I live'* & would I be able to run him there in *my* car? Again we went round the illogical houses, with me assuring him that at Inglewood was in *his only* current home, that he didn't have a house in London these days etc & so there was no home to go to that he wasn't sitting in already & that, sad to relate, his parents were unlikely to be still alive at 120-years-of-age..

So it goes some days...

So Ron's various delusions continue to wax & wane
according to the topsy-turvy snow-globe in his brain
& the curious meteorological flourishes of the weather-systems crashing around in his strange old mind.
There are clearer days & then cloudier days.

Even today he told me that he'd be going to New York tomorrow morning & returning the day after
& would I tell him which airline he was best to fly with?
He said he's going to be seeing *The President* for a meeting and sorting out some business stateside with his brother (sic) Graham.

2nd Oct 2016

On **Monday** Ron rang at 9.30am (Josie said he had wanted to ring me at 7am but she'd managed to get him to delay) to ask me if I knew anything about the extraordinary barometric conditions that morning. He was, he said, feeling as if something in the air was pinning him to the bed. I tried to distract him with news that my asthma is sometimes a little more challenging as summer turns to autumn etc... I think it was probably the result of one of those surreal dreams he is frequently at the mercy of - he talked as if some strange wind-god had clapped him in gale-force irons and pinioned him to his mattress...

Ron asked me to take him out to lunch. When I arrived at the apartment to collect him, Josie whispered - *'someone's visiting him - I don't know who it is.'* It turned out it was one Jean-Claude, a camp Portuguese waiter who used to work at Inglewood in the bar & restaurant. Apparently he struck up quite a friendship with Ron & used to chat to Ron & Mr. Brading (R.I.P.) in their former glory-days of holding court downstairs, in that hallowed corner of the Inglewood Bistro.

Ron invited Jean-Claude to join us for lunch, and off we went *a trois* to the Woodspeen. Ron seemed somewhat distracted & said that he really didn't like the noise in the restaurant
& that he'd like to find an alternative eatery, that despite the fact he'd enjoyed The Woodspeen on many occasions, his patience for the place was wearing thin.

It might just be his innate sexism: he certainly doesn't like it if he happens to be placed near a table of ladies-who-lunch and who are *'screeching'*.

There was something distracting Ron from having a good

time that lunchtime and I couldn't quite work it out. It later transpired that the reason was Jean-Claude.

Later in the week Ron told me that Jean-Claude was *'as queer as a coot'* and that if he had to see him again he'd *'get him jailed'*. It soon became clear that he'd taken against Jean-Claude's campness & Ron's old covert distaste for homosexuals was in the psychological ascendant.

Josie told me that Ron hid in the bathroom the following morning, when Jean-Claude popped in to visit again.

The only thing that bothered me was that Ron persisted in referring to JC as *my friend,* as if it was *my fault* that he was hounding Ron. I had to protest since I only met JC a couple of times, when he worked at Inglewood. The tragic thing, of course, is that JC, in his slightly queeny way, thinks that Ron adores him.... I'm not sure if this week's twists and turns ended up disabusing poor JC of this misapprehension.

Most latterly Ron told me flatly that *'Jean-Claude is an arsehole.'* So it goes in *Ronland.*

On **Tuesday** I went down to see Ron and pick up another dirty duvet - this time urine-rather-than vomit-soiled & took it to Hungerford dry cleaner. Ron was still in bed but we had a chat.

On **Wednesday** we spoke by phone, but I was at a funeral and a maudlin wake that day. The deceased was a friend & neighbour of my in-laws called John. Dead at 63. Only a six-month illness. Built his own house out here in West Berkshire & from scratch. An intensely practical man, who learned all the skills needed to self-build on land he had bought. Now his widow must live there in the House that John Built, all on her own.

Life is too short. It all just makes you think *Carpe* flipping *Diem.* As Nigel Tuffnell says in SPINAL TAP - *'too much flipping perspective, man...'*

By sad coincidence my favourite composer, Ben Britten, died at only 63. He still had at least 20 years of work to do. He was going to write the operas of KING LEAR and ANNA

KARENINA. Not to be. John's untimely demise reminded me how horribly soon Britten's death came.

On **Thursday** Ron rang asking, since it was another nice day, would I take him out to lunch again? I thought I'd better steer clear of the Woodspeen since he's decided he's gone off it and so took him to the Red House pub - which is slightly more difficult in terms of access - they have to open a side restaurant door to get the wheelchair up a steep ramp & in. Ron had prawn cocktail & fish & chips. The batter was pretty thick & I hacked it off for him so he could get at the white fillet lurking beneath this greasy, golden carapace.

On **Friday** I had a call from Ron to say that he'd had enough of Inglewood and had to move out as soon humanly possible (he didn't seem to know where) and said he was trying to get hold of you to ask for help. I said I'd pop in for coffee & chat that morning and did so - finding him on the phone to you in New York City. Ron was having one of his perennial downers that kick-in when Josie leaves and *'the Nidas of this world'* take over... i.e. he can't stand Nida & thinks she's *'thick as two short-planks..'*

I tried to get to the bottom of what was making him so dissatisfied with his life at Inglewood & gently suggested that he had it as good as it can possibly get for someone of his age & with his health challenges.... Distraction techniques are best on these occasions...

On **Saturday** Ron rang to ask if he should be ringing you again. I reminded him that you were in America and that it would be best to wait until the afternoon to try to get hold of you, due to the time difference. As you can imagine, most telephone calls are replete with deviation, repetition and hesitation such as would never get past Nicholas Parsons on Radio 4.

Today **Sunday**, as promised, I took Ron, with my son Thomas (8) to the Classic Car show at Shalbourne. We've been once before - it takes place on the sports field there & both Ron and Thomas enjoyed looking at the various automobiles and motorcycles. There were several Jaguar E-types which were rather beautiful - but a poor version of the wondrous machines you celebrate at your Windsor

119

Concourse of Elegance.

Ron seemed to really enjoy the afternoon - the autumn sun was bright again, a jazz-band played and I took him the scenic route home via Combe - a high escarpment affording lovely views across several counties.

10th October 2016

I'm off to New York for meetings tomorrow. Just went down to say cheerio to Ron. A3 OLD is sitting in the car park at Inglewood & nice Ian Crawford has the key.

Herewith a quick update on last week's adventures:

On **Monday** Ron asked me to take him to lunch at The Woodspeen. The patron John Campbell was there, incongruous in his shooting gear - off to shoot wild-duck in nearby Bagnor & said that we should give him fair warning of our arrival & he would cook us a fine *confit de canard*. (Ron said that he'd like to invite you down to sample it...)

I was running a bit late picking up the children - so decided to take Ron with me to school pick up & he seemed to love seeing the children rushing around at home-time
& Mrs Sanders (Louisa's teacher) had a nice chat with him - the playground energy is, of course, the opposite of the limping old crocs of Inglewood & seemed to invigorate Ron - a brief tonic - he's certainly always chatty & kind & curious with Thomas and Louisa...
On **Wednesday** Ron asked me to take him & Jocelyn out to lunch - so I found a new pub called The Pot Kiln - which he seemed to like - out in the bucolic fields beyond Hermitage - only problem being that the Venison steak he ordered (despite the fact that I asked beforehand) was too tough. He's finding even quite tender meet difficult to chew (and cut) these days... He particularly liked the melting chocolate pudding. He also enjoyed the extra attention of having Jocelyn by his side, of course...

Monday Ron asked me to take him out to lunch - so we returned to his beloved (& easily wheelchair accessible) Woodspeen. He's got the particular hots for that slim

Transylvanian waitress called Bianca. He's not too overtly-*Trump-ish* about it - but his eyesight immediately improves as she sashays by, carrying dirty plates...

I made one longer distance personal journey to Portsmouth (to visit HMS Victory - research for a Benjamin Britten opera called BILLY BUDD - my mentor Basil Coleman directed the first production in 1951) and to coach a young actor who was in the National Youth Theatre some years ago. He is now a Portsmouth bus driver - but he desperately wants to get back to acting & is doing some amateur shows on Hayling Island - but has had the stuffing knocked out of him after leaving drama school early & a toxic critical family destroying his confidence.. poor bloke... I'll see what I can do to revive his theatrical dreams...

29th Oct 2016

Just a quickie to say I'm finally back to Kintbury late tomorrow night from New York & Cornwall & Opera Philadelphia meetings in London - (first time I've flown Newquay to London) - actually really easy from Central London & makes *Kernow* very close - had a nice chat with Ron day before yesterday from airport & he sounds well - will pop in to see him on Monday - he says *"I've got a bottle of champagne for you, dear boy!"* Ian Crawford's been looking after him & took him to surgery the other day - which Ron reported was very boring & *all doctors are dodgy quacks...*

1st November 2016

Woodspeen for lunch today & right now at the retail park picking up groceries & incontinence pants - so normal service resumed!

6th Nov 2019

Back from New York & Cornwall & home in Kintbury late on Sunday night... kids conked out in the back & fished out of their seats in their pyjamas - the traffic is better setting off at 8pm
& avoids the constant arguments that ensue with 8-year-old & 5-year-old in close proximity. (I now realise what my

poor parents had to endure with the three of us & understand why they used to set off for my grandmother's house in Blackpool in those pre-seat-belt days, with the three of us lying length-ways in the back of the Vauxhall Victor. In time-honoured fashion we'd get to Richmond Bridge - 3 miles from home & say *'are we there yet?'.*)

On **Monday** (Hallowe'en) popped in to see Ron for a catch up & Claire and I took the children down post-village *Trick-or-Treating* so Ron could see them in their witch & skeleton costumes, which he loved.

Josie gave the kids some Proustian Madeleine cakes & (full financial disclosure) some loose change amounting to c. £2.

On **Tuesday** at Ron's request we ventured off to the Woodspeen restuarant for lunch. He's finding it harder & harder to bite into meat that isn't totally tender. This time he decided to go for the wild duck & then found it too chewy (it was delicious).

The only fly in the Michelin-starred ointment was the arrival of a party of ten women - the horror! - who proceeded to laugh a little too raucously for Ron's taste... I heard them in the bar as we arrived & thought this might be a concern... But Bianca the Transylvanian Waitress, to whom he has taken a shine, managed to distract him from his ancient-misogyny with some good old-fashioned sexism...
ever thus with the thoroughly unreconstructed Ron..

On **Thursday** Ron decided it was another nice day and he wanted to go out for lunch. I took him & Jocelyn to the pub we went to a few times in the summer - the Crown and Garter at Inkpen. He'd enjoyed sitting in the garden in the summer sunshine - but at this time of year we had a cosy round table by the open fire & Ron seemed very happy there. It's a good option this pub because wheelchair access is very good. It's recently been snazzed up by new management. (I spent my last night as a bachelor there in 2007 since it's around the corner from Inkpen Church, where Mrs K and I tied the knot.) Jocelyn was feeling guilty about coming along - felt that she should be ironing - but it's a nice distraction to have her there & her infectious laughter is a tonic at table.

Ron seems to really love the countryside hereabouts & it's putting on a rather beautiful autumnal display of colours that make the 23.5 degree tilt away from the sun (that happens each winter) seem divine rather than random....

On **Saturday** I picked up Ron's dry cleaning. Louisa (5) was in a strop & wouldn't go up in the lift & it wasn't worth fighting her. So Thomas (8) like perfect bell-boy, took the laundered jumpers up to the apartment & stayed for a chat with Ron & Josie. Good lad. Louisa is lovely, of course, but going through a particularly challenging stage...

My Claire was supposed to be singing two services at Clement Danes (Aldwych) today (Sunday) so we were meant to be driving A3 OLD up to town today. But she's been feeling out-of-sorts & cancelled - she had a bad time this week when a deer bounded out of a nearby forest & landed on her bonnet - causing much damage to the vehicle, death to the animal & not inconsiderable shock to my poor wife. The nastiest part of the event was that a couple of men got out of a van & started to berate her for, in a daze, staring at her broken bonnet, and not going to the immediate aid of the unfortunate animal. *'Women like you make me sick,'* said the idiots. *'Sorry, sorry,'* said Claire in her distressed state. *'It's no use saying sorry now, is it?'* replied the bastards. Fortunately nice people were there too & sprang to her defence & her critics departed, cursing. Some burly chaps from a local wood-yard dragged her car in & gave her comfort and support. (I must write them a thank-you letter.)

Oh, yes, life is red in tooth & claw out here in the sedate home counties....

p.s. Cast & crew screening of my movie in London on Thursday night this week... *EEK!*

13th Nov 2016

On **Monday** morning Josie rang to say that Ron had been tearful in the night & asking if she could ring me - I said I'd pop in to see him once I got back from my lunch meeting in Hampton Court - so I duly did & Ron actually seemed pretty chirpy when I arrived mid-afternoon...

(It's the perennial problem with night-time of course. His dreams take him to all sorts of difficult or toxic places in his psyche & then he finds it hard to wake from them, I think & his mind can't work out what is a dream & what is true.... more of which later...)

On **Tuesday** Ron asked me to take him to the Woodspeen for lunch we sat close to the kitchen & Ron enjoyed watching the chef Peter at his work with his *sous*-chefs - it's all very controlled & professional there & any bickering is kept backstage - so it's not noisy - the noise that most bugs chauvinist Ron, of course, is the sound of large-parties-of-Ladies-who-Lunch.

On **Thursday** first thing Nida rang to say that Ron was unhappily saying there was nothing in his life and he had nothing to live for. I said I could take him out for a drive & lunch & picked him up at 11.30am. We returned to the Crown and Garter in Inkpen...

We had a long discussion about the paradox that is Ron's belief that his parents are still alive. He started to say that he wanted to do more for his parents & that he needed to talk to you about ways you and he could look after them better. He affirmed his belief that his parents are still at 73, Ollerton Road in New Southgate. I gently reminded him that they died some time ago. Asked him if he remembered their funerals. Tried to take him through in logical steps the fact that, logically, his parents are no longer around.

We talked about the fact that he **knows** they must be dead - but somehow his mind won't let him **believe** it. His memory is so shot that it's hard to take him back through a sensible sequence of historical events.

I asked him if there were some sort of memorial gesture he would like to make, in memory of his parents. Make a donation to some charity.... set up a foundation or fund... Asked if that would allay the sense that he wasn't helping them since they couldn't be helped beyond the grave.

But Ron was adamant that he wanted to help them now, as they are, still resident in that terraced house just off the

124

North Circular Road.

He needed me to remind him again that Maggie was once his wife, but no longer. I took him through the story, as much as I know it, of he & Maggie divorcing & Henley days ending & the fact that Maggie remarried a man called Mr. Sharp, who has subsequently died.

Again, all this was a new mystery to him.

He told me that, the other evening, he'd been sitting in his armchair watching television
& the thought occurred to him that he should *'find Maggie, in the kitchen or wherever she is and take her to bed and have intercourse with her. She must be wondering what sort of bloody husband she's married'* - the inference being that he was neglecting his conjugal duties. He reported that he couldn't find Maggie in the kitchen...

I spoke to Maggie a few weeks ago & she reported that Ron had been estranged from his parents. That they were unhappy that he left your mother. That his gay brother Paul (of whose sexuality Ron had disapproved) had looked after them in their dotage. That his parents didn't meet Maggie until the day of your wedding. That throughout their marriage he would never say sorry & yet now, when he is calm, he is frequently apologetic.

But Ron can't remember these things....

But... Ron enjoyed **Thursday's** journey out & laughed a good deal & I drove him up to Combe Gibbet, the highest hill hereabouts & we looked out across four counties & then I ran him back down to his luxurious confinement at Inglewood.

That night I had the Cast & Crew screening of my movie at RADA in London.

Cripes it was SCARY.

On **Friday** morning Josie rang to ask if I could go to the GP and pick up a urine sample bottle which, on my return to Berkshire at lunchtime, I duly did. I delivered it to Ron. We

125

had a lovely talk about my film & the screening - which was UTTERLY NERVE-WRACKING - even the actors had never seen the piece before & in a theatre/opera project it's still possible to change things even after first preview... & in response to my story, Ron was animated & interested & kind & encouraging - as he so often is when the demons have loosed him from their nasty talons.

Then I went into a decline.
Probably the release of the tension after Thursday night.
Urgh.

18th Nov 2016

On **Wednesday** Ron asked me to take him out to lunch with Jocelyn so we went to The Woodspeen - Jocelyn's first time there. Much laughter at the restaurant & in the car. Ron on fine form & Jocelyn's infectious giggling soon enlivens him.

This week I made one longer-distance journey to leave the car at Ravenscourt Park when I went to English National Opera on Wednesday for a tribute to my mentor Jonathan Miller. It was a fitting celebration - he's worked there for forty years & created so many great productions at The Coliseum. I love seeing him always - but tragically his memory is really failing him now & Rachel (his wife) has to prompt him for even the easiest-to-recall name..

On **Monday** 21st I'm off by train to Aldeburgh. On Tuesday 22nd we have the 100th birthday of my other mentor Basil Coleman & there's an exhibition at Benjamin Britten's house The Red House & I will be making a speech & introducing some young singers from the Royal College of Music - who will sing pieces from two of the Britten operas (Basil directed their world premieres). In his will, Basil left half of the proceeds from his Barnes house sale (£2.2m) to Royal College of Music students to help them with their studies & half to Aldeburgh Productions to mount new productions of Ben Britten's operas.

I am now one of Basil's trustees/executors. A great honour. I have been asked to write Basil's biography. I really want to - but I need to raise the funds to be able to fund

126

my research - months of work. If any of your philanthropist friends happens to be a music-lover or, more specifically, an *afficianado* of Benjamin Britten's work - please could you put me in touch with them so I can send a begging letter! I would dearly love to be able to tell Basil Coleman's story - he was such a self-effacing man - but lived a fascinating life, working with all the greats of 20th century British Theatre & opera. He left all his papers to the Red House Library at Aldeburgh & it's a real treasure trove. I would love to be able to spend time properly working through it.

19th Nov 2016

Yes, you're right it's a conundrum re. Basil biography & raising funds to facilitate the time (so that I can still pay the mortgage etc). I would love to go to Aldeburgh & immerse myself in his papers & research - I'm sure I'll be able to write some kind of memoir - perhaps a collection of interviews with people who knew him - it'll just take a while. When the dosh starts to flow from my movies I'll be able to buy myself some more research time. Freelance careers (whilst not always lucrative!) are rich & various & you never know what creative seeds are being planted & where they're going to germinate. I have much to be grateful for & life teems with interest!

Next I want to make a movie about the death of Van Gogh. I'm convinced by the theory posited in a new biography- I believe he DIDN'T kill himself - but was shot by a teenage boy who was messing about with a gun. My movie will be the antidote to all that Kirk Douglas *Lust for Life* bullsh*t... That artists need to self-destruct etc.... The plot (& plotting) thickens! ONWARD!!

26th Nov 2016

Monday - Wednesday I took the train to Ben Britten's house in Aldeburgh, Suffolk, for the centenary celebrations for Basil Coleman. Terrific occasion & a fitting tribute to the man (though I say it myself!!). I did a talk with material largely lifted from the eulogy I wrote for his funeral and two wonderful singers from the Royal College of Music sang arias from THE LITTLE SWEEP and GLORIANA - accompanied in Britten's library by his own piano - operas

127

that Basil directed in their world premieres in 1949 & 1953 respectively. Since Basil's house in Barnes is no longer available - sold for £2.2m & major bequests given to RCM & Aldeburgh Music - it was great to be at Ben Britten & Peter Pears' house in Aldeburgh, which Basil knew so well....

5th Dec 2016

5th Dec 2016

On **Tuesday** I went to Inglewood & drank coffee & chatted with Ron while Josie had to go into Hungerford, something to do with getting cash out & petrol for her car.

It was then that Ron disclosed to me about seeing the Mother Elephant and her young *calf* (is that the right word?) outside on the lawn at Inglewood. As previously reported, I brought Ron his binoculars & said that if he spied the resident pachyderms again, he should ask Josie or Jocelyn to snap a picture on their mobile phones. As you quite rightly observe: he'll surprise us yet with a World Exclusive...

That morning Ron observed that it was a nice day & suggested another lunch outing. Seeking some variation in matters prandial; I had heard that there's a new Rick Stein's Restaurant which has opened in Marlborough & from the website it seemed to be wheelchair friendly. Jocelyn came with us this time. Parking is trickier in Marlborough – but since I had Jocelyn in tow, it was easy to drop them off & then go & park the car. The restaurant was less accessible than claimed & there's a temporary metal ramp (like something at a railway station) that has to be deployed up the stone steps at the front of the striking townhouse building that houses Rick Stein's new restaurant.

Ron ordered a whole Dover Sole and we enjoyed watching the waitress fillet the fish at the table before our eyes – great dexterity under observation. The only real blot on the landscape was that the room we were allocated (on the ground floor) was rather cold. I asked if we could be moved & they relocated us a couple of tables further away from the icy window. There was another room at the front with a wood-burning stove, which would have been ideal (but which was full). Ron was not best pleased & it was irritating that the place was chilly. He got rather grumpy & seeing

128

that Jocelyn & I were dipping our bread, Mediterranean-style, into our olive oil, turned his nose up and declared 'I WAS ALWAYS TOLD THAT OIL IS FOR LAMPS' & proceeded to order BUTTER for his bread....

He cheered up once the Dover Sole and new potatoes were inside him... but it was a shame that the place was made uncomfortable by temperature. The manager was very apologetic & offered us free coffees as recompense.

Sadly, as we returned home & were approaching Inglewood – two minutes away down Templeton Road, Ron said he felt sick & proceeded to vomit down his front. Poor Ron. We decided to keep going since we were almost on the Inglewood drive. Jocelyn shot into the building and up to the apartment to get towels etc. Poor Ron very apologetic about his sickness. We got him up in the lift & into the warm & Jocelyn changed him. Straight away I took the car to the car wash to be cleaned, as the seat belt & carpet were slightly soiled. I went back later to see Ron & check he was feeling better.

12ᵗʰ Dec 2016

Along the way this week, Ron reported that he's p*ssed off with Maggie's constant visits & her moaning & wanting to watch his television & drink his champagne... She'd like him to put up the Christmas wreath she's given him for his apartment door & has asked if I'd find a nail & do it. Ron says he doesn't even want *the bloody thing*... so it goes...

On **Thursday**, Ron said he wanted me to take him to buy a Christmas Tree & so we drove to Cobb's Farm (local farm shop) & spent £40 on a rather handsome, freshly-cut tree. We took it back to the apartment, but Josie said we needed to buy a base to stand it on/in. (I'd thought there was something at the apartment from last year.) I said I'd go to the garden centre & find one - BUT Ron insisted on coming out with me again. We arrived at the garden centre and, in helping him into his wheelchair, poor fellow, he said he felt rough & seated in the wheelchair, proceeded to vomit between his legs onto the car park tarmac.

I asked for help to clear up & the nice folk in Costa Coffee brought Ron a bottle of water. I took him straight home to Josie's care to recover. The doctor later called to see him at Inglewood. I'm not sure of the cause of his recent vomiting attacks. On this occasion it wasn't as if we'd just been for a large lunch.

I went to B&Q at the retail park & bought a rather ingenious Christmas Tree base which has a clasp & lock which secure the tree in an upright position - this can be re-used annually & has a water-reservoir to keep the tree a little fresher as it dies & tragically sheds its needles (despite its demise being mocked by a plethora of gaudy baubles.. are we not a cruel race?)

....The previously purchased pull-ups were Boots own-brand - which Josie tells me are inferior to the famous Tena Men brand (WHO KNEW??) & so I got a refund on that purchase & bought new pull-up pants...

(Sadly, second childishness is coming to us all, Graham. From infants-in-nappies to Tena Men in a few short decades...)

That evening Ron rang me on his mobile to say 'I DO NOT REQUIRE THE EMERGENCY SERVICES.' I'm not quite sure why he thought he had to do this. I told him he was phoning me & not the said services & steadily talked him down from any putative emergency footing...

On **Friday** I went to Inglewood at 9.30am to receive Harry, the washing machine man, who duly arrived & with the requisite spare valve, gave me a (somewhat inappropriate given his surroundings) lecture on his belief in euthanasia, whilst effecting the repair.

Josie had had a bad night with Ron. He was up in the middle of the night, locked in his bathroom & banging with his hairbrush on the sink, making a loud sound. Josie was worried this would disturb the neighbours.

The logic seemed to be that he was feeling hot, was running the cold tap & rinsing his hairbrush, then running it through his hair to try to cool his overheated head. But then, somehow, he kept banging the hairbrush on the sink, to get

130

rid of excess water. And then getting trapped in some fugue state.... which meant this course of repeated action went on for some time.

I had coffee with Ron that morning & he was in some distress about it - said he was patently losing his mind and asking what could be done by the medics to save him from these nocturnal delusions. I tried to reassure him that the incident with the attempt at cooling his head was actually a logical thing to do & the problem was his memory sometimes got him stuck in certain looped situations....

I said that we were seeing you this coming week & we could perhaps talk about doctors & treatments & what further help there might be...

Josie said that Ron had been swearing at her in the night, telling her to 'F*** Off etc...' She looked a bit drained but said, patiently paraphrasing the Nazarene Carpenter: 'It's not his fault, he doesn't know what he's doing'.

Later that day I had a cuppa with Ron & he opened a Christmas Card from old Henley friends. The picture was of a fisherman crouching by a snowy river and having no luck in catching anything. Behind him, Santa is kindly slipping a large salmon into his keep-net. Ron remarked that Christmas Cards of late had certainly deteriorated in quality and subject matter. Referring to the crouching fisherman, Ron said 'he looks like a bloody great Arab with a bomb.'

12th Dec 2016

12th Dec 2016

Just to keep you informed - had a call from Nida at 8.45pm saying that Ron had fallen & she couldn't get him back in his chair & could I come & help...

Have just been down - Ron was sitting on the living room floor in front of his chair. He said that the small of his back was hurting. His food tray had gone flying & a glass was broken. I'm not sure how exactly he fell. Nida had sat him up on the floor but couldn't get him up to his chair.

We got him into his wheelchair & then to rest on his bed & persuaded him it would be a good idea to take a couple of paracetamol. Before I arrived, Nida had said she would phone for an ambulance but Ron really didn't want that & asked her to call me. I did ask if he'd like us to get a doctor out to see him - but he didn't want that. I left Ron lying on his bed with a cushion under his back & calm.

I've got my phone on overnight if I need to go down again. I'm not sure what the story is with Inglewood staff coming up to the apartment to help if emergencies happen. There seems to be an emergency button - but Nida didn't know if it was to be used - I am unsure the protocol. If I don't hear overnight I'll ring in the morning & check how he is.

Sorry to bother you & don't mean to worry you - but feel it's important to keep you posted immediately with any Ron health situations.

13th Dec 2016

FYI just rang Nida - she reports that Ron had a peaceful night & no nocturnal wanderings...

18th Dec 2016

Good to see you this week - such a shame poor Ron wasn't well that day & plans had to be curtailed. Do hope we get the chance to take him to Thatcham to see those wonderful motors of yours before too long...

On **Tuesday** Ron asked me to take him out to lunch, so, since I knew we were going to the Woodspeen later in the week, I took him to the Three Tuns pub in Great Bedwyn, which has a good reputation for food & which we hadn't tried before. Ron ordered scampi & chips & got half way through it, but then felt unwell & so I took him home.

On **Wednesday** Jocelyn told me that Ron had been complaining about not being able to see the fairy lights at the bottom of his tree - so I bought an extra new set of lights & an adaptor...

On **Friday** after school we went down with the children to see Ron after the last day of term. The children went into school wearing Christmas jumpers & were keen to show

132

them to Mr. C. Thomas also showed Ron some sewing he'd done, a miniature Santa stocking & Ron said *'I'm not sure I approve of boys being taught to sew!'* I remarked that sometimes men made excellent tailors.

Ron insisted on putting a £5 note in Thomas's little stocking. He then drew my wife aside & said he was worried that he hadn't given any money to Louisa & would we split the funds between them - which we duly did. I later had a discussion with Thomas about the older generation's views on gender roles etc & how sometimes elderly people were set in their ways etc! Josie (in the kitchen - where Ron seems to think she chiefly belongs...) gave me a shopping list to take to Tesco...

On **Saturday** Josie rang to ask me if I could phone & talk to Ron. Apparently she'd been having real trouble convincing him that he didn't live in London any more & that he shouldn't be trying to get home. Josie said that Ron had been insisting on ringing me from 2am onwards. Josie managed to keep him from doing so. I rang back to speak to Ron but did not have good mobile signal (I was at the library in Hungerford with the children). When I rang back later, Josie told me that Caroline had rung & been able to talk Ron down from his delusional mission to get back to London....

******

FESTIVE WEEK

On **Tuesday 20th** Josie rang in the morning to say Ron was miserable & wouldn't get out of bed & was there a chance I could go down & see him. I went down about 3pm & had a couple of hours with Ron (haven't felt confident to take him out to lunch in last couple of weeks due to the sickness he's experienced.. which you'll remember....) That day Ron was very keen to tell me that he'd bought a new apartment in London & that Maggie would be waiting for him there. It's a second-floor apartment that overlooks Hyde Park (!) - there's basement car parking... I tried gently to disabuse him of this delusion... but he was holding onto it tenaciously...

On **Wednesday 21st** I picked up a prescription for Ron from Kintbury Surgery & went to Boots in Hungerford to pick up the antibiotics. At 12.30pm Ron was still in bed. As Josie requested, I drove to the Mobility Store in Marlborough to buy incontinence pads & gloves & aprons etc. When I took this down to Inglewood, stopped for a cup of tea with Ron & he told me, very earnestly, that he had been outside the building, pacing out the measurements & that he was waiting for a surveyor to come with professional measuring gear - as he wanted to demolish much of the block & rebuild it, with slightly larger rooms.... (!)

I put the Christmas presents under the tree & stayed for an extensive tutorial with Ron about his recent London house purchases & his marital status. He was very keen that I take him over the road to the house he shares with his wife Maggie... etc etc... tried again to remind him of true status of things... hard going, I'm afraid....

On **Tuesday 27th** Nida rang at 2.30pm to ask me if I could speak to Ron because he had become obsessed with the idea that Maggie was waiting for him in his London house & he needed to be taken home & didn't know where he was. We talked *'around the houses'* for some time. I tried to calm him down by saying that I didn't know the address of his new London flat & that I would have to find that out & then get back to him.

That morning it was noticeable that Ron was up betimes - I was there about 9.30am & he was happily sitting in his chair in the living room. Many times, under the auspices of Josie & Nida he has not been out of bed when I have popped in at noon. Jocelyn said that sometimes the district nurses (who administer morning injections) had complained about this. She also thought that this might contribute to Ron's sickness - that not getting up in the morning was contributing to spikes in his insulin that could lead to nausea etc.

From my untutored perspective it does seem that Jocelyn is able to get Ron into a better day/night routine. Both Josie and Nida have complained of late that he will be up all night, calling them every 20 minutes or so & then will sleep from early morning. But, believe me, I don't underestimate

134

the challenge of their various tasks, so wouldn't want to be seen to be standing in judgement. Just keen to keep you informed, however incomplete my understanding of the full situation...

******

Jocelyn said that she & her husband John had taken Ron out for Christmas Day Lunch at a pub in Hungerford & he'd had a nice time & hadn't been unwell (great news!). She showed me a photo of Ron looking very chirpy wearing a Christmas-Cracker Paper Crown....

I can't thank you enough for that wonderful hamper from Harrods. I've never been given anything like it - wonderful - & the box will be an excellent storage resource once I've indulged & emptied the contents. We've already drunk the claret! *Yum.*

Thank you to you & Emma for your many kindnesses in the last couple of years since I met Ron.

I can't tell you what a help it's been in so many ways & a real privilege that you have trusted me to look out for your dear old Dad.

Merry Christmas!

C IS FOR COLLUSION

ME:

So, Ron, you're feeling like you've had
enough of this place?

MR. C:

I'm not feeling, dear boy. It's got to the
stage where I *should* escape.

ME:

Yes. And where would you escape to?

MR. C:

I don't know. That's the problem.

ME:

Yeah..

MR. C:

I can't escape by myself. No. I need help.
But that's not the point.. the point of my
exasperation –

ME:

Yeah..

MR. C:

.. has been in bed –

ME:

Yeah..

MR. C:

.. feeling well –

ME:

Yeah..

MR. C:

.. as well as reasonable..

ME:

Yeah..

MR. C:

Of course if I get up, I can realise I'm
still very weak.

                              ME:
Yes.
                         MR. C:
But that's obvious –

                              ME:
Yes –

                         MR. C:
And that's going to be so – and it's not
going to stop me wanting to escape –
                              ME:
Yes, quite, yeah..
                         MR. C:
Sorry, boy, to bore you with this..
                              ME:
Not at all, no..

2017

To: Graham Clempson
Subject: Driving Mr. C

Hi Graham

Happy New Year to you & Emma.

Took Ron to the Woodspeen for lunch. He ate heartily and had a lovely time. John Campbell (the boss) materialised & made a kind fuss of Ron - Happy New Year from all the staff & a tiny cake with a candle in it & Happy Birthday written in chocolate on the plate etc...

Yes - a grand time & Ron seemed very happy. He's still particularly taken with Bianca the Transylvanian waitress, who features prominently on the Woodspeen website, *natch*.

John Campbell also said that he can get Ron a better deal on the Ayala Champagne than the one he currently has from Naked Grape wine merchant in Hungerford. He told me to get in touch next time Ron needs a new order. It was at the Woodspeen that Ron first encountered & enjoyed that particular brand of fizz.

Later from Josie I heard the bad news that disaster had struck. Soon after I had dropped him off, Ron was copiously sick. Such a shame.

On **Friday** I took dry cleaning to cleaner in Hungerford, including that lovely blue jumper you gave Ron for his

138

birthday.. (he had been sick on the sleeve..)

I had a long, non-sequitur-filled, talk with Ron that day about rich food & his intolerance for it. He was very disappointed that he was unwell after the Woodspeen. I have suggested that we could go out again & only have one course & perhaps forgo alcohol...

On **Saturday** Jocelyn reported that Ron wanted fresh flowers (they tend to wilt relatively quickly in his necessarily warm apartment)

Jocelyn looked pretty washed-out. Apparently Ron had been up since 2am saying that he had to ring me, urgently... *Oh dear.*

When I saw him, Ron told me that he wanted *me* to sack Nida & I told him I was only a humble driving operative & that hiring & firing was beyond my pay grade (tugging my chauffeur's cap the while...) He also said that he'd never met Nida, so, as per usual, there was a slight lack of consistency in his logic.

I made two longer-distance personal journeys the first to leave the car at Ravenscourt Park tube - took the kids to the South Bank for a walk & a ride on the carousel & to see the amazing African Limbo dancers. (Sounds like Dr Johnson's London, not New Year Bank Holiday 2017.) Yesterday I drove Thomas to Calne in Wiltshire where his Under 9s football team was thrashed 14-1 by the locals. All very character-building, allegedly. Poor lad. *Beautiful game,* indeed.

Josie did (independently) say that when people get older their ability to tolerate complex food can be compromised etc - but it would be good not to have to axe our excursions...

10th Jan 2017

Forgot to mention longer-distance journey last Sunday to Evensong at Winchester Cathedral - wanted Thomas (8) to see the choirboys his age sing - but turned out the lads weren't back in their choir stalls till next week. Nonetheless the cathedral organ is pretty impressive when the bass pedals kick in & we had seats in the *"quire"* & Jane Austen's skeleton is under a slab in the aisle... *culcha's* everywhere, innit & only had 70p on me to put in collection box. Bargain.

11th Jan 2017

Pleased to report we went to Woodspeen & Ron home now & not feeling unwell. None of us had any alcohol. Ron drank water. He had two courses - no dessert.

15th Jan 2017

I spoke to Jocelyn in the morning & she said that Ron had been shouting abuse at her that he wasn't going out & that he was going back to bed. She was worried that she wouldn't be able to get him up in time to leave. I arrived at 11.30am & he had calmed & was perfectly polite to me & Jocelyn was getting him ready.

At lunch, Ron asked Jocelyn if he'd been to his *new* apartment. *The one opposite the park.* I wasn't sure if this was the new one opposite Hyde Park that we'd talked about previously - but he says this one has a view out into the trees. Never quite sure if he's actually referring to Inglewood, or some mental coagulation of various other locations when he talks in this way...

On the way to the restaurant, I saw a sign to the Thatcham Sea Cadets and said *'Ron, you used to be a Sea Cadet, didn't you? Or was it a Sea Scout?'* He wasn't clear either way - but suddenly perspicacious about it being the Southgate & Potters Bar Troop... so it goes. These moments of great clarity, poke out like peaks seen from altitude, from the general clouds of forgetting....

On **Friday** I took Ron & Josie to Thatcham Community Hospital where Ron had a chest X-ray. I gather the results will come through in about a week. Fortunately Ron didn't have long to wait to be seen - which was a relief, as you will attest, he often finds his patience wearing thin in hospital waiting rooms...

140

23rd Jan 2017

On **Monday** had a message from Josie to say that Ron had been awake 12am until 4am & wanting to ring me. I rang at 9.30am in case he wanted to go out - he'd been talking about wanting to buy a new coat - but this didn't happen that day... I think he was too exhausted after his disturbed night...

On **Wednesday** I took Ron to the menswear department at the Newbury department store called Camp Hopson - he's bought clothes there before & it's easily accessible with wheelchair. Ron bought a navy-blue winter coat - said £149.50 on price tag - but ended up being zapped at the till for £99. He was pleased at the sniff of a bargain...

Thereafter took Ron to Woodspeen for another lunch. I managed to keep him off the champagne - but let him have one glass of the red *Chateau Viramiere* he has always enjoyed there. Initially he was getting grumpy about the noise levels - you'll remember that the design there is a resonant concrete floor - Scandinavian chic I suppose - but this means that the surrounding conversations are louder than they might be. Once he'd had a glass of wine he seemed to mellow... He ate well & John Campbell (Le Patron) came to see him & gave us a chocolate pudding that they are *'trialling'* for the new menu & Ron seemed chirpy & said - *'what a wonderful lunch'*. He wasn't sick then or thereafter & I rang Josie to check later & she said he was fine.

The main thing I'm really pleased about is that Ron had a good time at the Woodspeen & ate three courses - but I engineered limiting alcohol intake to one glass & if we can keep it at that level I hope it won't again trigger the nausea. He does so enjoy getting out - he's now a real celebrity at the Woodspeen - that I'll be glad if he doesn't have to dispense with those excursions.

On **Friday** I popped down to see Ron - Josie said he'd been on the go all night - wandering the hallway corridor & opening and shutting cupboard doors. She follows at a safe distance, suggesting that he goes back to bed, but this can lead to him becoming more confrontational...

In the morning he had no memory of these nocturnal roamings... Jocelyn has found a baby monitor in a charity shop in Hungerford which Josie was proposing to set up to connect the two rooms.

When I got back we had a good chat... I told him all about my day in London & he enjoys this glimpse of the Big City he knew so well, I think...

I made two longer-distance personal journeys. The first to leave A3 OLD at Ravenscourt Park Tube & then to Shoreditch for a meeting with my designer for WRITTEN ON SKIN - the opera I'm directing next year at Opera Philadelphia. From there to Camden for tea with my old mentor Jonathan Miller - sad to say he's losing his (once phenomenal) memory too... and then in the evening I went to a brilliant production of MARY STUART at the Almeida Theatre (highly recommended!) - which was, in fact, the theatre where I was Jonathan Miller's assistant director in 1996 & the reason we got to know each other...

29th Jan 2017

On **Friday** I took the car to the car wash & then chauffered Ron & Jocelyn to the Woodspeen Restaurant - only slight bore was a large party of Friday lunchtime young execs (Vodaphone HQ is nearby) having loud lunchtime laughs. The acoustics in the Woodspeen - concrete floor rather than carpet & glass & wood - mean a loud table can disturb others.. & Ron was in a bad mood about this. He even said *'I've never liked the food here'* - which I know is not true!

30th Jan 2017

Picked up Maggie from LHR bright and early this AM...
She says she never wants to pack & unpack a bag ever again.
At New Year - disaster! - the first Phuket Hotel, called SLATE, was, *well*, made of slate.
Dark & cavernous & all the staff were wearing (modish but deeply depressing) black. Pretty soon Sarah's husband decided they should all decamp (unpack/pack/unpack) to a much nicer luxury hotel the family has stayed in before, so the day was saved.

Oz with her bro in Cairns was WAY TOO HOT & humid.
Talking of Australia - darling Roger Federer is a god. Isn't it
great that he's won The Open? & BTW there's NO
WAY Andy Murray should have been given a knighthood.
The honours system is utterly debased... they hand them
out like sweeties now.... What an AWFUL man that Andy
Murray is....and his mother is even worse..... etc etc...

In short: Maggie was much happier once we'd stopped at
the Kintbury Corner Store and she had a real *print* copy of
the Daily Mail, bless her. The iPad version just isn't the
same...

Now a whole host of new worries crowd in upon her... she
needs a new phone with a bigger keyboard & what to do
about the car? etc... I've said I'm happy to ferry her hither &
yon... It's a hard-knock life... But, the main thing is, thank
God she's survived the far shores & is back in Civilisation -
(a.k.a. West Berks).

3rd Feb 2017

On **Wednesday** took Ron & Josie to Royal Berks Hospital
in Reading... went to the back door that Josie showed us
last time... (when you were with us.. saves the hell of the
multi-storey car park the other side)... Josie took Ron in & I
drove round & around & eventually found a parking space.
Ron in a foul mood when I found him & Josie on the ward -
cheesed off with waiting around & about to go home -
'What a dump,' he said... *'I'm never coming back here, you
can be sure of that...'* We managed to get him to wait to be
seen... luckily a nurse came & said *'you're next in the queue'*
- just in time to keep him from insisting on storming out..

Off Ron went to see the specialist - and then you'll be aware
of the next part of the story - some kind of lens was found in
his eye.. the last few days he's convinced himself that this
was some kind of conspiracy to blind him & he now needs to
go back through his medical records to find out exactly
which quack-charlatan was responsible. He seems to think
there's some ocular Harold Shipman out there who is going
around depriving unsuspecting patients of their sight... He
plans to SUE the BASTARDS.

143

Delivered the shopping to Inglewood & had another chat with Ron. He reminiscing about gas masks & the Bombing of Ollerton Road... strange to think that Ron was my Thomas's age (8) at the outbreak of WWII.....

By the end of the week, I will have made two longer-distance personal journeys. On Tuesday I drove the car to Ravenscourt Park tube station & left it there & went by tube to English National Opera because Jonathan and Rachel Miller had invited me to the morning dress rehearsal of Jonathan's production of RIGOLETTO, which is having its umpteenth revival. I sat next to the actress Dame Penelope Wilton - an old friend of Jonathan's since she played Cordelia for him at Nottingham Playhouse (to Michael Hordern's KING LEAR) when she was only 22. Hearing this, my mother-in-law was more impressed because she's recently starred in Downton Abbey.

The RIGOLETTO is set in 1950s New York among the Italian mafia community. It still works as a concept, in fact, but that's enough revivals now methinks, time for a new production from a younger director (much as I love Jonathan & have a lot to thank him for.. not least my introduction to working in America ten years ago this year...)

12th Feb 2017

On **Sunday** 5th at 9.30am Jocelyn rang in tears could I come down & talk to Ron he was being so horrible to her & so abusive & she couldn't take any more etc - I went down for an hour - Sarah the nurse came - Ron calm & contrite when I arrived *'it's my cracked brain'* he said & said he'd apologised...

On **Monday** picked up a urine sample to take to GP & chased up the antibiotics - but they had been delivered by Boots with Ron's other medication.

On **Tuesday** Ron rang to say he needed money & chocolates (bare necessities for us all). Jocelyn there & they were getting on well & laughing.

Took Ron to Woodspeen Restaurant where he had a lovely

time. John Campbell the chef-patron appeared & made a fuss of Ron & said he would bring us the new *Tarte Tatin* for dessert. Noise levels not too bad from other tables (no braying Vodaphone executives this time) to make Ron grumpy. He abstained from champagne at lunch but had one glass of Chateau Viramiere (the red wine he likes to drink there). No nausea - though some post-prandial indigestion as per usual. Ron weaker this time getting in & out of car, but these strength levels can wax & wane.... Sometimes he stands from wheelchair much more easily.

(He reportedly found superhuman levels of strength when pursuing the late-lamented Nida around the apartment, waving his stick above his head....)

Ron rang several times on **Friday** suggesting that I had rung him (I hadn't).

.... drove to visit my parents in Hanworth. My Dad's dementia strangely less evident yesterday - he even asking occasional questions & volunteering answers to mine .... tiny shades of his former chatty self... but only fragments...

How I miss his old incorrigible/annoying/loveable identity, which has been so horribly eroded by the *Curse of Alzheimer*.... so it goes...

20th Feb 2017

Stop Press:
A call from Josie at 12.30pm today to ask if I could give Ron a ring as she couldn't get him out of bed. He being very grumpy & aggressive - telling her she's nuts etc.... I said I'd pop down the road & duly did & of course Ron's always sweetness & light to me... *'Come in, dear boy!'* - the problem is he's needlessly on night-shift/New York time again - banging around through the small hours & finally crashing out at 6am (by which time whoever's the carer will be at the end of their tether) & then sleeping till noon...

But it seems to be enough of a change of gear that I pop in & bring him his *Financial Times* & have a cuppa with him at his bedside & thereafter he becomes placid & amenable...

145

24th Feb 2017

On **Monday** Josie rang at 12.30pm to ask if I could ring Mr. C to calm him down. She couldn't get him out of bed & he was being very agitated/abusive/angry... I said I would go down to Inglewood & Ron as ever passive & apologetic. Still in bed. Jocelyn seems to be able to get him up & dressed & in his chair much more easily than Josie, for some reason. Josie said Ron had been up all night till 6am & then conked out till noon & then been out of sorts & protesting at her 'interference'.

We had a talk & coffee for an hour or so. All calm when I left & Josie able to get him dressed etc.

Delivered the shopping with Thomas (8) having dropped Louisa (6) at her ballet class. Thomas is studying World War II & it was just great to see Ron talking about his experiences during the Blitz & about evacuation... Thomas listening intently. Weirdly enough, Thomas is exactly the age Ron was at the outbreak of WW2. Ron always lovely with the children...

Yesterday I had a few hours free between school drop off & school pick up & made this week's one longer-distance journey, to the Pallant House Gallery in Chichester. They currently have an exhibition (highly recommended) of the Australian artist Sidney Nolan (this year is his centenary) & a terrific permanent collection of British Artist's paintings - including Basil Coleman's friend & colleague, John Piper.... The gallery was started with the art collection of Walter Hussey - a famous clergyman patron of the arts who commissioned music & art from the composers (including Ben Britten) & artists of his day. I popped in to Chichester Cathedral & there were other works Hussey had commissioned when he was The Dean - a Chagall stained-glass window, a Graham Southerland & Patrick Proctor paintings of biblical scenes - John Piper tapestries etc. Oh & found grave of Gustav Holst (he of *The Planets* fame) didn't know he ended up there & the twelfth-century Arundel Tomb - Philip Larkin wrote a famous poem of that title inspired by the couple holding hands (in effigy) on the tomb... a fascinating day.. & then back to school gates just in time to pick up the Little Tyrants...

146

3rd March 2017

...Ron back to his (good old) grumpy self (he was worryingly weak when I took him out to lunch the previous Friday - could hardly get his fork to his mouth, shaking hands & complaining that the cutlery was too heavy) but that day he set to moaning about the standards at the Woodspeen having "fallen 500%" (they really haven't).

Had a good chat about taking the quacks to court & how it's taking a while to collate the evidence - but when we get to the High Court we're going to take them to the proverbial cleaners & most of the NHS eye-specialists will be banged up in Wormwood Scrubs for the foreseeable..

On **Tuesday** morning I took some of Ron's jumpers to the dry cleaners in Hungerford. At 10.30am (unexpectedly) Jocelyn rang in tears saying that Ron was being abusive towards her
& asked if I would go down to Inglewood. I arrived at the same time as Anne-Marie the nurse & listened to a distraught Jocelyn. She said that Ron had been bashing his stick against the table in his bedroom, threatening & swearing and telling her to get out & shouting that she was ugly & making racist & generally abusive remarks.

Ron was immediately compliant on my arrival & passive with the nurse Anne-Marie as she administered his injection. Thankfully, Ron was *Dr Jekyll* & not *Mr. Hyde* again - but a bruised Jocelyn asked me to stay while she got him dressed in case things kicked off again....

I waited in the living room & then Ron came through & we drank coffee together... Ron was calm & as per normal but, but confused & when he vaguely remembered some indistinct conflict, regretful that he thought he'd been shouting at someone...
(he couldn't work out who had been the target of his ire...)

On **Wednesday** Ron rang & left me a message (from his mobile) saying that he'd been reading the *Financial Times* & didn't trust that bad lot Green (he was referring to Sir Philip Green who has done a despicable number on the BHS

pensioners...) & wondered what my take was on the story....
(not a very informed one...)

Hilariously, on Tuesday, I'm off to the Royal College of
Music, in my capacity as a trustee of Basil Coleman's Estate
(he bequeathed them a lot of money from the sale of his
house in Barnes) for a prize-giving concert/private
reception & (I think) will have to shake hands with H.R.H.
Prince Charles.

This is actually the second time I've met him. I had to
do the same in 1995 when I was an assistant director on
Walton's TROILUS & CRESSIDA at Covent Garden &
HRH came backstage & I was in the line-up. Being
neither vehemently republican, nor vociferously
monarchist, I thought I was looking him in the eyes &
shaking his hand like an (almost) normal bloke - but if you
examine the photographic evidence, I was doing the full
Uriah Heap – a maximum-toady-cringe. Oh well, we shall
see if (despite myself) I kick into grovel-mode again on
Tuesday morning....

11ᵗʰ March 2017

On **Wednesday** picked up dry cleaning from Hungerford
Laundry & had coffee with Ron & regaled him with stories of
my day at the RCM shaking hands with HRH - hilariously
they treat me like a major donor because I'm one of Basil
Coleman's executors & whilst I'm **not yet** a millionaire
myself, Basil's gift of £1.2 million set up in trust as the Basil
Coleman Opera Award means that I get to ride on his
posthumous glory.

Poor H.R.H. - what a miserable job to have to make
conversation with all these dull toadying people for whom a
handshake with him is a biographical highlight... they say
that the Queen must think the world smells of fresh paint &
it must be the same for Prince Charles. Give him his due, he
looked utterly downcast, but lit up when awarding prizes or
interacting with people. A strange study in the behaviour of
high-status people - they don't have to do to much to retain
their status - the power comes from the way we forelock-
tugging underlings react to them....

148

Ron very amused by my tales of rubbing shoulders with royalty...

13th March 2017

Forgot to mention in my report that on Wednesday I took a sample of Ron's wee to Kintbury GP. I'm not sure whether that resulted in yet another prescription of anti-biotics, but Josie keeps copious medical notes & will know full story.

Life is rich and various.
Last Tuesday I was shaking hands with HRH Prince Charles (& trying not to take the p*ss.) And last Wednesday I was taking the actual p*ss - in my official role as Urine Courier to Lord Clempson of Inglewood.

20th March 2017

On **Saturday** Ron rang in a state of great confusion - couldn't work out who Maria was or what she was doing there - spent a while on phone trying to calm him down, reassuring him that she was his new carer etc & that she'd been trained up by Josie & all was well.... He seemed to take notice, but pretty muddled...

On **Sunday** popped in to Inglewood with the children in the afternoon - the kids, of course were angelic with Mr. C - Louisa demonstrating her ballet poses & Thomas telling Ron all about the football match that morning (& no mention of the fact that earlier I'd completely lost my rag with them...)

Jocelyn rang me to ask if I could come back as Ron was in poor state of mind, telling her she was fat & ugly & thick & uncivilised - *'Who are you anyway?'*... went down to see if I could ease situation... Ron calmed down & ate his lunch & I left to do school pick up leaving a more peaceful atmosphere at no. 7.

27th March 2017

On **Tuesday** a message from Ron to ask if I'd take him out to lunch - off to Woodspeen - Ron drank both champagne & wine & no tummy troubles & particularly enjoyed the

Chocolate Torte pudding...

On **Wednesday** ...chatted with Ron - he said he was very keen *'to go to The Hut to visit Josie...'* - couldn't quite work out which "*hut*" he's referring to...

On **Thursday** another distress call from Jocelyn at 2pm - apparently Ron had been complaining that his food was cold & anyway she hadn't supplied him with 'a menu' before the meal etc... unfortunately I was off to London for meetings so couldn't come to the rescue on that day...

On **Friday** Ron rang on his mobile sounding a bit confused... but I was able to big-up Maria who was looking after him that day & say that he was in safe hands etc etc & that Maria had been well-trained by Josie...

I think he likes Maria because he sees her as better-looking than Jocelyn. Somehow Jocelyn has morphed into his perception of Nida - whom he never liked & therefore ended up treating her with considerable disdain... & Jocelyn's pretty thin-skinned about it.. whereas Nida used to be more combative... tricky... but I gather from Jocelyn that she's been talking to Caroline about these local difficulties...

I made two longer-distance personal journeys, one to Ravenscourt Park tube on Thursday, going in to Royal College of Music to see a Handel opera called FARAMONDO - in my role as Basil Coleman's executor. Strange that these days we sit through all three hours of these interminable Baroque operas these days - in Handel's time, audiences were free to come & go & would have returned in time to see their favourite *castrati* sing favourite numbers - & cheer for their heroes more like a modern football crowd....
& then on Friday I drove to Oxford for meeting with composer Andrew Gant. He is writing a new opera for me to direct next year in Cromarty based on Beatrix Potter's THE TALE OF MR. TOD. It'll be a world premiere & very exciting prospect. We had a fun afternoon, reading the Beatrix Potter story & thinking about best ways to stage the story - quite a challenge - little kidnapped bunnies trapped in ovens & older rabbits burrowing under the house to try to rescue them & a massive kitchen-wrecking fight between Tommy Brock (the Badger) & Mr. Tod (the wily Fox)...

150

Tomorrow I'm taking Maggie to Henley for a ladies' lunch (don't have to stay this time so off on pilgrimage to John Piper's grave/stained glass windows at Fawley).

28th March 2017

See below - really pleased that artistic director Paul Roseby's asked me to do a new project with NYT - directing scenes from TWELFTH NIGHT in the place where it had its First Night in 1602!!

...do take Emma to see THE KID STAYS IN THE PICTURE at The Royal Court - she'd enjoy the story of the crazy movie business - not least because of her Pa's involvement in the biz...

2nd April 2017

On **Friday** I picked Ron up to take him to The Woodspeen for lunch. We got to the restaurant at 12.30pm but sadly, Ron was sick in the car just as we arrived. Poor Ron. He hasn't been sick like this for some months & this was BEFORE he had had his lunch (of rich food) at the Woodspeen.

I quickly went into the restaurant to tender my apologies & cancel the lunch booking & swiftly took Ron straight home to Maria. When I got home Maria rang & said she had booked an appointment at the GP & would I pick them up at Inglewood at 2.30pm, which I duly did.

Took Ron to see the Kintbury GP - lots of hanging around waiting to be seen, I'm afraid & he was given more medication & then I took he & Maria home. A great shame if Ron is back to being sick again. He seemed to have left that unpleasantness & discomfort behind in recent weeks.

On **Saturday** I took the car back to the car wash to clean the interior after Ron's unfortunate mishap.

I made two personal longer distance journeys, the first to Ravenscourt Park to leave the car when I went in to London for meetings. The second to the RSC at Stratford on Friday

151

night, where I saw Richard Bean's new play THE HYPOCRITE in the Swan Theatre. I directed a play by Richard Bean called THE GOD BOTHERERS in 2003 at the Bush Theatre & he's since become very successful & rich (ONE MAN TWO GOVERNORS London/Broadway/Tour) & so it's good, of course, to get back into his orbit & going to his plays is a politic way to do this... & tweeting about how wonderful his work is...etc...etc... (!)

The car is stowed in Inglewood Car park - I was about to say 'safely stowed' but this is debatable when most of the old crocs of Inglewood probably should have given up their driving licences long ago & there have been several cases of prangs in the car park with overambitious reversing, poor spatial awareness & arthritic feet slipping from brake to accelerator pedals.... so it goes...

20ᵗʰ April 2017

An exhausted Jocelyn asked me if I'd take Ron out the following day. That was also the day we went down *en famille* & gave Ron one of Louisa's special Easter Cards.... Jocelyn enjoyed talking to Claire in the kitchen & sharing her troubles.... *'It's so nice to talk to another woman etc...'*

On **Tuesday** morning, Jocelyn rang in tears saying that she was having a hard time & asked if I'd come down to help. I had the children (still school hols) & couldn't help just at that moment & suggested ringing you.

Today, **Thursday**, Jocelyn said she was running short on Ron's incontinence pants & disposable gloves so would I go to the mobility store in Marlborough?

I made one longer-distance personal journey with the family to Fleet Street on Good Friday, where Claire was singing Stainer's Crucifixion at St Bride's (I love driving in the City of London at Easter when it's empty) & then we went on to a friends place in Beckenham where various singers and their families were convening for garden barbecue etc & then home to Kintbury.

25th April 2017

Ron left a message at 7.36am today to ask me to take him to lunch .. so that's the plan...
I tend to go with the Woodspeen by default because Wheelchair Access there is so easy
(& other places hereabouts tend to have ramps or steps etc...) & they know the state of play & bring Ron crustless bread etc & make a polite fuss of him...

Meeting with a potential new Opera Agent in London tomorrow & hoping I like him.
Hopefully when my film eventually comes out I'll be able to get a movie agent... we shall see!
As you know they can be useful for keeping contract negotiations at a distance (but are fundamentally flesh-eating succubi who take X percent of fee plus VAT for any work you (of course) create yourself...)

2nd May 2017

Do hope all well with you & Emma & you had a good Mayday Bank Holiday.

In Kintbury, we had the traditional English Patriot Morris Dancing (presumably beloved of the EDF) in the village square, followed by Theresa May's Young Fascists (including our Louisa (6)) dancing around the Maypole in the field behind the Coronation Hall. Roll on Brexit & the expulsion of all the Johnny Foreigners & let's get those saintly Blue Passports back... Hurrah!

(Or alternatively thanks a bunch to the *Daily Mail* Reading Old Gits for making it much harder for me to direct operas in Europe & for my children's generation to travel & work freely across the continent... my foolishly-idealistic-dilettante-lefty-artistic-tree-hugging-pacifist-anti-nuclear-vote will be wasted again in this True Blue Stronghold on the 8th June... Heigh ho..)

On **Tuesday** I took Ron to The Woodspeen (he calls it our 'Club') for lunch & had a happy time on day-release from Inglewood (Alcatraz with added £££££).

153

On **Friday** I had a message in the evening from Maria asking if I could go to the surgery the following morning to pick up more urine sample bottles, as she suspected Ron was suffering from another infection of the urinary tract.

I'm off to Edinburgh tomorrow for two nights - meetings with designer about this year's Cromarty Youth Opera show - entitled ELEPHANT ANGEL & set in the Belfast blitz of 1941 – based on a true story about a young zoo-keeper called Miss Austen who took a baby elephant home each night during the bombing raids... we have to make an elephant puppet - shades of the National Theatre's WARHORSE etc...

Just spoken to Ron & since it's a nice day he's asked me to take him out to lunch - just booked table at his beloved Woodspeen.

3rd May 2017

Nice lunch with Ron yesterday, though he was particularly keen to hear if Claire & I were married by a vicar & if I knew a friendly local one, *as he thinks Josie & he should have a church wedding... (!!)*

8th May 2017

Ron was very keen to ask me about the possibilities for Josie & he having a church wedding. He couldn't remember if he'd had a church service with your Mum & thought it was a registry office affair with Maggie - but this time he said he'd like to get married in church & asked which vicar had married Claire & I & had it been local etc etc. I'm not entirely sure of the current state of canon law - but told him that he might be able to get a blessing & that the civil part of the ceremony would probably be dealt with at a registry office before any church service. Though times have changed & perhaps divorcés can get spliced in church these days.... Ron said that he felt he was probably C. of E. - though he didn't sound very specific about his beliefs in the divinity of Christ or the nature of the after-life...

On this occasion, I didn't really feel like saying 'WTAF Ron? Josie is YOUR CARER, man!!! - she's freaked out by any

154

suggestion of romance between you & she - what in GOD'S NAME makes you think she'd want to marry you...????" ...and, anyway, such an intervention would have unsettled him & have spoilt a rather convivial lunch he seemed to be enjoying.... some days, discretion really is the better part of valour...

That evening I left the car at Inglewood & the keys with Josie & went to Edinburgh Wednesday to Friday for meetings about ELEPHANT ANGEL (new show for Cromarty Youth Opera this summer). I gather that nice Ian Crawford had done a couple of errands in my absence & no doubt he'll have been in touch with you directly about those. Sad to hear from Josie that Ron had been sick on his bedclothes & Ian had to take soiled things to Swift Laundry in Hungerford while I was away...

On **Friday** Ron obviously had some bee in his bonnet & rang me about ten times on his mobile & after my meetings I was able to reassure him that all was well & I would be back 'Down South' (as Scots tend to disparagingly call England) shortly...

On **Saturday** morning I popped in for coffee & a catch up. Ron spoke rather movingly about his great affection for 'my' car & how it had been so very reliable & how attached he felt to it & that he'd never felt quite this way about a motor car before & how the great service A3 OLD has given him should not go unmarked & perhaps there was some way of recognising the car's long & valuable service? I'm not sure what he has in mind, perhaps there is some sort of M.B.E. for motor-cars in the parallel universe that is Ronsworld. I opined that, yes, the Audi represented freedom & noted that Ron always enjoys his trips out & the chance to see the local countryside & escape from the apartment....

It's probably best if defer writing to the Honours Committee in Whitehall & asking if there is some valedictory medal offered to motors for outstanding service. (They might think I was some vexatious satirist, or deluded Berkshire Nutter & ignore my correspondence...)

I have, however, with your blessing, booked the car in for an M.O.T. at Newbury Audi on Thursday & hopefully the

155

mechanics will give it some T.L.C. to reward it for being such a very good & well-behaved automobile... On arrival at destinations, I often pat the steering column, equine-style & thank it for a pleasant journey & the nice Albanians at Hungerford Car Wash are unstinting in their care & attention, so perhaps the OLD Girl feels the abiding love that we all have for her...

9th May 2017

The new debit card arrived this morning & I've just been at Inglewood- trying to guide the point of Ron's biro to sign it - quite a tricky procedure even without his sight/motor problems...

Your Dad on good form today so we are off to the Woodspeen for lunch - currently at Car Wash & lavishing Albanian attention on Our Heroic Motor... A3 OLD - G.O.S.T. (Grand Order of the Squeegees of Tirana)

15th May 2017

Herewith an update on last week's adventures - a busy week with various *curve-balls* (as I believe you say in America) or *googlies* (sp.?) (as I think we say this side of the pond) to field...

Ron to the Woodspeen where he had the salmon starter he always loved & then I thought he'd be safe with the Sea Bream & Jersey Royals (potatoes) that he had last time & seemed to relish. Pretty soon into said main course, he looked disgruntled & then said he never wanted to come to the restaurant ever again, vowing never to return as long as he lives.... (??!!) Not sure how to play this. He'll probably forget. A shame because it's so easy from an access/understanding point of view. Might try taking him to the Crown & Garter Pub again because this is next best option for accessibility. Though he is annoyed that they only do prosecco by the glass & not proper champagne...

So we left without making it to the dessert course.

On **Wednesday** I popped in with the children after school - they have sweetly learned to ENUNCIATE (shout) if they

156

want Mr. C to be able to comprehend their tales of ballet & football etc... nice to see him light up in their company - the old twinkly-eyes-sparkle etc...

I had a plaintive message from Josie saying that she'd hard a bad night with Ron & he was complaining about none of his trousers fitting him & would I help him to buy some more. I decided that it was best to pick up several pairs from Camp Hopson's menswear department & take them back to Inglewood, so Ron could try them on at home. It would be a practical challenge to try to get Ron in & out of fitting rooms etc as I have done formerly, since these days he is much more immobile & invariably having to use the wheelchair - best to take trousers to him for trial....

On **Friday** I picked up the post-audition-trousers - the 40" waist fitted, but not the 38". I exchanged two pairs & commissioned the alteration of all four pairs spending £48 to have the legs shortened (you can't get a 40" waist to match Ron's not-extensive inside leg). Later, Maria rang to say that Ron was in a state of agitation, saying he needed his car to go to London & would I ring? When I had a chance to phone a little later, he had forgotten all about these urgent transportation requirements....

On **Sunday**, I picked up the altered trousers & delivered them to Inglewood. Ron's *Tag* (I'm assuming it's a fake one as per the others) had stopped working & so Jocelyn asked if I could take it to get a new battery fitted. She was worried that Ron would be fixated on having his watch back ASAP. I went back into Newbury but nowhere that was open on a Sunday would do a while-you-wait service...

(Today, **Monday** I have just returned from Timpson. The man there couldn't fix it just by renewing the battery- says it needs a service. It's been sent away for further attention from their watch specialists. The Timpson man said he thought it was a real Tag, but I'm assuming, from your previous statements, that all Ron's classy watches are fakes via Sarah-Jane's shady horologist-contacts in Hong Kong....)

16th May 2017

I'm at swimming lessons with my kids but just wanted to let you know popped in to see Ron beforehand & his speech a bit slurry & leaning to one side in his chair. When I saw him his speech pretty confused but not distressed. On phone GP advised Josie to get paramedics to see him & they're currently checking him over. Have just checked in with Josie again & Caroline is on phone & had spoken to paramedics.

Just wanted to keep you immediately posted...

21st May 2017

On **Monday** I took Ron's watch to Timpson & they sent it away for repair. I later contacted them to ask if they could expedite the repair because it belonged to an old man who would be unsettled by its absence. They considerately agreed to process the work as an urgent repair. There is kindness in all sorts of people.

On **Tuesday** Josie rang to say that Ron had had a very bad night, had ripped the buttons from his pyjamas & removed his pyjama trousers & therefore pads & had wet the bed. She asked me to buy new bed protectors & pyjamas & to take the soiled duvets to the dry cleaners. This was the day on which he seemed rather unwell when I went to see him - lolling slightly in his chair & slurring his words. Caroline spoke to him & the paramedics.

As always, don't want to worry you - but if there was even the slightest chance of some sort of mini-stroke having taken place, I feel it my duty to keep you immediately informed. Your dad continues in his strangely Teflon *always-bouncing-back* manner... which is always good to see...

On **Saturday** Josie said that Ron had become agitated & angry about his missing watch & the day before (when I was holding NYT auditions in London) I had a message from Timpson to say that the watch was ready for collection. I picked it up on Saturday morning & delivered the watch to Inglewood.

... went to see my mentor Jonathan Miller in Camden Town (who is steadily losing his memory... such a shame to see such a huge intellect felled like some Great Oak condemned...)

..... auditions at NYT for my TWELFTH NIGHT project - performance at Middle Temple Hall - we are the after-dinner entertainment for an assembly of lawyers from the Inns of Court - much as Shakespeare's players were in the same venue in February 1602... I auditioned 25 excellent young actors & only really have space to take 24 on the project... tough for them & a tough choice for me as they were all very promising young performers... need to decide tomorrow...

.... Ron who seemed on pretty good form again, sitting in his chair, sporting a salmon pink shirt, pressed & clean... awaiting the arrival of his daughters.... I do hope they have a nice time.

26th May 2017

On **Wednesday** - a very sunny day - Ron said that he would like to go out for lunch. Decided to take him to the Crown and Garter, because last time I took him to his (formerly) beloved Woodspeen Restaurant, he had decidedly taken against it & said that he never wanted to go back there *as long as he lives*.

The Crown and Garter is that nicely refurbished village pub with a long & picturesque garden. Ron, Child of Helios that he is, decided he wanted to sit in direct sunlight & even asked to be moved as the shade (of the old oak tree behind him) inched across his face... I tried to steer him in the direction of the fish & chips he's had there before and enjoyed, but he was insistent that he wanted the fish pie & proceeded to hate it. Oh dear.

But he was out in the sun in a nice pub garden. Took him for a bit of a drive up the hill to Combe Gibbet - where you can see several counties laid out before you from the top of the hill where the para-gliders roam - all those bored Newbury Accountants throwing sickies at the sight of the

159

sunniest day of the Financial Year & launching themselves off that steep escarpment in a vain attempt to break the surly bonds of earth & escape from their cursed spreadsheets etc. In 1944 Eisenhower was here with his paratroopers & they used the rolling hills in the area as practice jumping grounds for the fearless parachute-men of the Normandy Landings.... there's a time-worn plaque to that effect...

Ron seemed to enjoy his escape into the countryside, even if he found the lunch unimpressive...

On **Thursday** Josie said Ron had been complaining about the flowers in the vases at Inglewood. Poor things don't stand much of a chance of flourishing in the old-person's-apartment-Kew-Gardens-Hothouse-temperatures that hold sway at Inglewood & now with the heat o' the sun in addition, they are doubly damned. Went to Tesco bought various compact blooms - Carnations are pretty indestructible, though not, I confess, to my taste.

Ron wasn't on great form that day, I'm afraid. He was having his lunch very late when I turned up about 4pm. Josie said he'd not been faring too well on the new medication he'd been prescribed... I didn't stay long..

5th June 2017

In between times yesterday I took Ron to lunch. Since he's recently taken against The Woodspeen (he'll probably not remember) I took him to The Vineyard - the Relais & Chateaux place we've been to a couple of times before. I think it's way too pretentious & the actual cooking doesn't justify the expense or the *up-itself*-attitude... though the waiting staff are all very pleasant.

There were a hundred spelling mistakes in the Bar List - so, like the vexatious pedant I am, I asked for a pencil & did some proof-reading for them. They'll probably hate me. It's supposed to be a 5* hotel. But seriously - you don't spell strength '*strenthg*'.... or puritan '*puritain*' ..... or chocolate '*chocolat*' (unless you are French) or camomile '*chamomile*' unless you are American *or* French...... & somebody teach them the *muthafunking* rules about how to use

160

APOSTROPHES...

Poor Ron didn't feel like talking - *'How's Josie,'* I asked & his reply was: *'Who is Josie?'*.... - so the spelling corrections gave me something to do in lieu of constructive conversation...

After much prevarication & confusion over the set-menu (Sunday Lunch 3 courses at £39) Ron & I ordered the roast beef & pork respectively. The kindly (rather posh & portly) young waitress made the mistake of trying to offer Ron a straw when she saw him trembling as he lifted his water glass to his lips. Previously, playing nanny, she'd given him a different-shaped glass for his champagne, when she saw him struggling to lift the tall thin glass to his lips at an ever-more acute angle....

The Incident of the Drinking Straw did not end well, I'm sorry to say:

                    MR. C:
A what?
                    WAITRESS:
A straw? Would you like a straw, sir?
                    MR. C:
A WHAT?
                    WAITRESS:
A STRAW - a drinking straw?
                    MR. C:
A STOOL?
                    WAITRESS:
A straw...
                    MR. C:
WHAT? A STOOL????
                    WAITRESS:
A STRAW, SIR.
                    ME:
Thank you - I think he's probably fine...
                    MR. C:
A STRAW?!! NO - I DON'T WANT A STRAW!
                    WAITRESS:
(exits table right) Okay ... sorry...

            MR. C: **(to me)**

```
A bloody straw?  What the hell is wrong
with the service at this place?  A STRAW?!
'course  I  don't  want  a  bloody  straw
(etc...)
```

Ron picked at his starter but then, when his main course was presented said he didn't want it. He said he'd rather go hungry than eat anything at that table.

It was soon time to go home. When we got back I told Josie that he'd eaten next to nothing & she said she'd make him a meal.

A shame that it was one of those disappointing occasions when Confused/Surly Ron is in Residence... I took the executive decision to leave a large tip for the poor beleaguered waitress. They didn't charge us for Ron's meal.

Pleased to report that ENTER THE DRAGONS - the show I co-directed for a company called A&E Comedy has just won an award at the Brighton Fringe Festival - I'm thrilled for the two actors - here they are in this picture - with their trophy - looking drunk & delighted...

12th June 2017

On **Thursday** I popped in to see Ron. He was still in bed mid-morning but seemed pretty chirpy, if confused.

13th June 2017

Truth to tell, I don't think there's such a thing as a stress-free job of work. I'm on the train to first rehearsal with the same nauseating nerves that always kick in (however small or large the show)...

23rd June 2017

Last week I was rehearsing for THE GULLING OF MALVOLIO - our NYT filleting of TWELFTH NIGHT for performance at Middle Temple Hall, where the play had its world premiere 415 years ago... a great project - a big success & talk with Paul Roseby of doing the whole play there one day.... I'm very pleased... the actors only got half an hour in the actual hall to run through the piece - but I tried to train them up so that they were a crack team of cultural paratroopers & could swing in & play the show anywhere & they rose to that challenge like real troopers... good for them... great young talents...

I stayed with old friends in Chiswick whilst working on the play - but came home for one night on **Saturday** & popped in to see Ron & Maria for a catch-up that evening...

Ron called Maria & I together in the living room for some kind of meeting - but I wasn't very clear what the import of it was - but King Lear-like, it had definite surreal shades of a Clempson Properties boardroom lecture of decades ago...

I was back home in Kintbury on **Tuesday** & went down to see Ron who was on pretty weak form that day - Jocelyn having trouble getting him to eat anything much at lunchtime... really not himself... seeming pretty weakened by the heat.....

I plan to take the car to Aldeburgh, Suffolk this coming weekend because I am giving a talk with Humphrey Burton about my mentor Basil Coleman & his directing the first production of Britten's BILLY BUDD at Covent Garden in 1951 & for the BBCTV in 1966... A real privilege to be able to talk about the self-effacing Basil & his work... They're having the first ever performance of BILLY BUDD at Snape Maltings (Britten's concert hall) that night & I get a free ticket...

Shame Claire can't come to Suffolk for the weekend, but we just can't sort the requisite childcare to enable such a mutual escape. In April, when we went away to Nice for two nights for our tenth wedding anniversary it was a logistical marathon.... & involved the cashing in of several hundred thousand Pixie Points with the in-laws....

....anyway the kids are growing fast & soon they'll be far gone & we'll be pining for the current level of responsibility of having a 6 & 9yr old...
& crying over old photos of exactly this period of family life.... so it goes...

25th June 2017

Back to Kintbury tonight from Aldeburgh - terrific performance of BILLY BUDD at Britten's concert hall Snape Maltings last night - my mentor Basil Coleman directed the world premiere in 1951... the music & story powerful & alive as ever, even though its creators have gone...

3rd July 2017

On **Wednesday**, Josie rang saying Ron needed some cash to pay his chiropodist. Picked up his debit card from Inglewood, made a withdrawal from the cash machine & delivered the dosh.
Had a long chat with Ron before the foot-woman turned up.

Ron said he'd been wanting to see me.... very keen to have a meeting about our *End of Year Results* & how the balance sheets are looking & what sort of profit margin is manifest?
& could I report to him my future projections for growth of the business in the coming financial year? & how our Business Plan is shaping up? etc etc...

Well... I said.... that's really all rather above my pay grade & suggested he talk to you
& said that I wasn't party to such intelligence regarding The Company's stock market
activity & the rising & falling of his investments etc etc...
(help!!)

Tried to explain that I was given the privilege of using the *Magic Debit Card* & that the account that draws on is always healthily in credit... though not quite sure I managed to give Ron the information he was seeking about the well-being of his financial assets & Clempson Investments Inc....

Then the chiropodist turned up & saved me......

6th July 2017

Stop Press:
Pleased to report that I **DID** get to drive Ron yesterday - had an unexpected call in the morning from Josie saying he'd like to go out. He seemed brighter than he's seemed for

a while (though very weak in the legs for getting in & out of car) & took him off to Woodspeen - hoping he'd forgotten that at last visit he'd said he NEVER wanted to go there EVER AGAIN.

We had a lovely time & Ron ate heartily & was full of praise for the place & John Campbell (The Patron) came & made a fuss of him & welcomed him back. Ron was happily much more talkative than he's been of late....

The last few weeks he hasn't seemed strong enough to go out at all,
so I'm pleased to see he's bounced back *yet again*...

8th July 2017

On **Wednesday**, on Josie's instruction, I picked up some medication from Kintbury GP. On delivery, I was very pleased to hear that Ron had been asking if I'd take him out that day.

We haven't been out for lunch for several weeks, to be honest I was feeling like that part of our connection was fading away, Ron has seemed so much weaker in recent months.... but no... off we went to The Woodspeen- Ron's only disappointment being that Bianca, the slim waitress he likes to watch working the tables (!) was having a day off. He was somewhat confused, but actually on good form & making non-sequitur-filled conversation & actually ate well, despite the indigestion & the odd thunderous sneeze into his napkin. John Campbell (the patron) came to see him & all was well. A surprising & pleasing return to form and no mention of the fact that the last time we went to the Woodspeen he opined that he would NEVER darken their doors EVER again & that the restaurant had been good once but now, it was a dump & .... NO WAY etc etc....

On **Friday** morning I popped in to see Ron:

'Ah, dear boy... come in.... can you help me?
I just want to know, Will, are my feet still on the ground?'

I replied in a puzzled affirmative - a mode much-deployed these days...

I made one longer-distance personal journey - to Chiswick with my wife Claire to go to Arts Ed drama school - for the retirement party of our old friend Jane Harrison who, in the last 16 years, has completely turned the school around from p*ss-poor ratings, to being one of the top-rated London drama schools. She's also been a brilliant fundraiser & managed to get c. £3,000,000 out of Andrew Lloyd Webber to build a brand new theatre.... Good old Jane. I hope she'll be able to actually switch off now - she wants to spend much more time with her adored grandchildren & is thinking of selling her Chiswick High Road home & moving to Hackney to be nearer them - but I can't imagine someone as driven as Jane ever just *ligging* about...

12*th* July 2017

Thanks so much for the dosh & the Ibiza Health Farm update - you must be feeling RAVENOUS if it's only lentils & yoga down with *"da kids"* on Love Island..

I've sporadically tried the dreaded 5/2 diet but it just means I'm a grumpy b*stard for a couple of days a week & wake with a spring in my step & a huge craving for sugary porridge & toast with a ton of butter on the days when the torture relents...

Talking of abstemious living - Ron fancies going out for lunch - so it's dry rusks for two at the Woodspeen today...

Joking aside, it's good to see him feeling fit enough to find the energy to want go out on day-release from his luxurious detention unit...

All best & I wish you a swift return from that horrid health-farm to bacon-bap-world...

17*th* July 2017

Do hope all well with you & Emma
& you've had a good time in Ibiza **(THUMP THUMP)** on Pete Tong Island...

On **Monday** picked up prescription cream from Kintbury

GP from for poor Ron's chafed botty.. Took it to Inglewood for coffee & chat with Ron...

On **Wednesday** Ron said he'd like to go out to lunch again (!) so took car to car wash & chanced the Woodspeen... Ron wouldn't eat his sea bass (main course). I think it was too artfully presented & when he's taken against something... *'no way, no way'* - then it's pretty much case closed... he was disappointed to hear that his favourite waitress is on maternity leave.... (he did put away salmon starter & ice cream dessert & some cheese even if he disdained the poor (delish) fish)

That evening Jocelyn rang to say that Ron was being particularly difficult again - shouting sexist abuse at her etc & was there a chance I might come & intercede. I was already in my pyjamas so didn't go down to Inglewood to fire-fight - but rang Ron & tried to distract him & that seemed to work...

On **Friday** I had lots of silent calls from Ron on his mobile & several chats *'My mind's gone, Will...'* he said...

23rd July 2017

On **Monday** morning went down to Inglewood & had a coffee with Ron - he wanted me to talk him through his various medical conditions because *'you, Will, are The Controller'*....(?!)

On **Wednesday** I went down to see Hugh the Dishwasher Repair man into the apartment.
I had coffee with Ron while Hugh successfully effected the fix. Josie said that Mr. C needed more cash & drew me aside confidentially to tell me that Ron had insisted on giving Jocelyn £100 in cash to thank her for all she did the day before - the trip to Sussex? I'm not sure if this is true. There's an ongoing animus between J & J & I try to steer a course between both...

......I had a call from Ron, asking if I'd be prepared to drive his car from time to time, as he was concerned that he was finding driving more & more difficult.... (!) I said, of course, I'd be delighted to assist....

167

24th July 2017

Ron asleep both times I popped in first thing this morning mid-afternoon....

24th July 2017

I'm staying the night at my parents' house (they live near Heathrow & it's an early flight up to Inverness tomorrow morning) feel like I'm about 12 years old - early to bed, back in the old bedroom with the telly blaring out below me...

And suddenly I'm 52 & 12 simultaneously
& realising how very fast this life is going...

I'm off to Bonnie Scotland where there's a simple reason it's so green - RAIN!!

14th August 2017

Just a quick update to say I'm back from Scotland & my show with Cromarty Youth Opera - all went well.

We popped in *en famille* on Saturday evening for a quick drink with Ron - he was on good form.

16 Aug 2017

re. memory quacks... I've been in attendance before on such occasions - bitter-sweet when Ron can't remember the date - or the name of the current Prime Minister (wouldn't we all rather forget her?)

Maggie thinks her beloved Jacob Rees-Mogg is soon to take command of the government & declares, despite my quaking at the prospect, in her best Orwellian tones: *"Oh Will, you will learn to love THE MOGG!"*

On **Saturday,** back from week's work with British Youth Opera in London, went down to see Ron. He very happily ensconced in his comfy chair & watching motorcycle-racing on telly.

...Went down to Inglewood for 9.45am & had coffee with Ron & was in attendance at appointment with Mary the Memory Nurse. She conducted the customary battery of tests. In the kitchen (out of Ron's hearing) was able to talk to her honestly thereafter about Ron's variable conduct & memory problems. Mary gave Jocelyn & myself a form to complete - various questions about Ron's condition & behaviour. She then went through with Jocelyn Ron's various medication, making copious lists etc.

In conclusion, she recommended no further change to his medication & praised Jocelyn for her sterling work etc.

Jocelyn asked me if there was a chance I could take Ron out - he was on good form today & had suggested an excursion. Since the car was at the garage I decided to take the executive decision not to seek out a courtesy car (for one day), but to accompany Ron to lunch at the Inglewood Bistro, where he spent £68.14 on lunch - I signed (pp) the bill in his stead.

He was on pretty good form - though he did, at one point, ask me if I knew of any other restaurants hereabouts, so that he didn't have to eat *'this muck'* (what seemed to be rather appetising scampi & chips, in fact, to my untutored eye.....)

4th Sep 2017

Arrived home from family hols in Nice on **Wednesday**. Spoke to Josie on **Thursday** morning - who said that Sarah-Jane had visited last weekend & that Ron had been particularly tricky thereafter - something to do with being jealous of Maggie, to whom he'd subsequently been rather beastly... she also said she'd been having great trouble lifting Ron from chair to bed to chair etc & that his legs were very weak..... & that it had been necessary to ask for extra help - I gather someone else was in attendance last week....

Went down to see Ron for coffee that morning (made it to Inglewood before our French postcard to Ron did - I noticed it on his hall table today)

I shared my Nice tales with Ron & talked about the euro being (an exorbitant) *94p-a-pop* against the pound - the added expense of which meant that I was cooking quite a lot of pasta & fish fingers in the Nice apartment, rather than taking the kids out for supper the whole time... (post-*Brexshit* vote & subsequent turbulence, this fall in the pound was only to be expected, I suppose...)

(My wife Claire is singing at the Opera House of Monte Carlo in the spring whilst I'm directing at Opera Philadelphia - with the pound so weak it's probably a good idea if we can earn as much as possible in €€€ & $$$, I suppose....)

Josie said that Ron thought I was taking him for lunch.... his legs were particularly unstable & was worried about getting him in & out of the car - so just went down to the Inglewood Bistro for lunch. He was deeply apologetic rather than irascible this time, said that he didn't care for his lunch & that he must be ruining mine with his objections & that he couldn't taste anything - (though he did some fair damage to a nice piece of salmon & potatoes & peas and, I thought, actually ate characteristically heartily....)

Took Ron back to the apartment & he returned to bed - stayed around for a while in case Josie needed a hand with manoeuvres. Later heard that he hadn't stayed in bed for a siesta after all & got up soon after I departed...

Josie gave me a shopping list so I headed off to Newbury Retail Park & groceries at M&S & Boots - for incontinence pads/razor blades/un-perfumed baby-wipes etc...

Late that evening I'm afraid I missed a call from Maria. I listened to the message the following morning & it was her asking for help with Mr. C who was being somewhat obstructive. We were having a little party to celebrate Claire's new CD release that day & so I'd had a couple of glasses of fizz & didn't check phone.

I spoke to Maria on **Saturday** morning & she said that Mr. C had in fact, soon calmed down the previous evening. I popped down & had coffee with Ron & he seemed on fine form.

This morning - **Sunday** - I was peeling potatoes & had a call

170

from Josie to ask if I could help her. Ron was sitting on the low chair in the living room & ordering her to move the furniture around - saying that he needed to completely redesign the layout of the flat & configuration of the furniture & generally being quite hard-to-handle.

I went down to see the lie/lay of the land. Ron, at my arrival, was not so concerned about the furniture - only suggesting that he needed to move the television from one end of the room to the other (!) - but that this task could wait. He did, however, give me chapter & verse on how he was going to completely restructure the gardens, needed to get excavators in to level a couple of hills which were concerning him & to plant new trees to obscure the tractor (!) & various other pieces of heavy machinery he'd been preparing to deploy.

Not altogether sure why Ron's landscape-gardening alter-ego, *Capability Clempson* came to call today.

I went along with this & said I'd help him to alter interior layout & garden features in due course, when his notions had fully crystallised for the redesign. He seemed to buy this & I toddled off home to crisp up my roast potatoes for Sunday lunch *chez nous*.

4th Sept 2017

I'm about to pop down to Inglewood & see Ron for coffee - he's currently in bed having been up for much of the night. (I've just spoken on phone to a weary-sounding Josie).

Ron abed while I was there so we tiptoed round with kitchen/bedroom door closed for washing-machine repairs. He didn't stir. He's been pretty weak of late - mobility greatly reduced by little strength in his legs.... so, sadly, no excursions to report.

15th Sep 2017

On **Wednesday** I spoke to Ron mid-morning & said I would pop down to see him but when I did he had fallen asleep again, so didn't disturb him. I picked up the laundered jumpers & delivered them to Inglewood.

In the evening Josie rang to say that Ron was experiencing chest pains and would I come down and help out by ringing 111 etc (the story has a happy ending, so I didn't bother you at the time).

I went down to Inglewood. Josie said that it wasn't an emergency - but she thought Ron should have a visit from a doctor. It was after 6.30pm so both Kintbury & Woolton Hill surgeries were closed. We rang 111 & answered a battery of questions. They told us an ambulance was on its way. After a while a pleasant ambulance-woman arrived (she'd been on another call at Inglewood) & did a series of tests on Ron & was with us for about an hour. She said there was nothing acute to worry about - but did notice that Ron's blood sugars were low. On her advice, Josie gave Ron a piece of toast. He settled back to rest soon after & I returned home.

I rang first thing in the morning on **Thursday** to check how Ron was & Josie said he was fine - he's going through a period of not sleeping too well at night & then sleeping on and off for much of the day.

I spoke to Josie this morning - **Friday** - who was changing guards with Maria. Ron alright but still abed. I picked up the laundered duvet from Hungerford laundry & delivered it.

19th sep 2017

Saw Ron for coffee yesterday & he very buoyed up by having seen you at the weekend.

Stop Press - just had a message from Jocelyn saying that Ron would like to go out for lunch!
She's going to come with us - easier getting him in & out of car if there are two of us. Wheelchair access so much better there than any of the pubs hereabouts & they always make a tremendous fuss of him. Though Ron's favourite waitress, the Transylvanian Bianca, has moved on to second maternity... He will be disappointed not to see her sashaying through the tables... All things pass....

24th Sep 2017

On **Monday** popped in to see Ron - he was in bed but chirpy after your weekend visit - when I asked him who had come to see him he said *'Oh, you know, the usual people - it was lovely'..*

On **Tuesday** Jocelyn said that Ron had said he'd like to go out for lunch. Jocelyn volunteered to come along & so we were able to go out rather than staying in downstairs bistro & we went off to the Woodspeen where Ron had a really happy time & ate heartily.

I also drove to Bath to my dentist (argh!) & on to Sutton Coldfield for rehearsals with B'Opera - an opera company that makes shows specifically for very young children - (0-2 yr olds) this one is called I CAN SING A RAINBOW & is about the dreary RAIN meeting the buzzy SUN & falling in love & making a RAINBOW... as I was eating my pre-rehearsal pad Thai in a local restaurant - marvelling at the strong midlands accents around me & thinking how strange it is that a few motorway junctions can change dialect so thoroughly & the most amazing & complete arching RAINBOW burst across the bright grey urban sky.... a good omen for the project, I think....

They are making me a token payment for my artistic advice at a couple of their rehearsals this time, but hope to raise funds to afford my enormous directing fees for a full production in the future... In truth, I just love the *variousness* of the broad church that is opera & theatre & my work is, of necessity, a case of being invited out to play and mostly saying yes...

Jocelyn is back tomorrow so might see if we can take Ron out together again. I am most wary of taking him out on my own at the moment because Ron's legs are particularly weak & I don't want to risk him falling as I try to get him in or out of A3 OLD. But he really did seem to enjoy his escape to the Woodspeen for lunch this week.

Do hope this finds you happy & as busy as you'd like to be. Maggie said she loved seeing the pictures of your house in the USA. Sounds like you & E, L & S are finding it a land of

173

fun & opportunity. I must say America has always been very good to me & I have found the legendary *'can-do'* attitude to apply wholeheartedly in my field of work. I got so sick of the UK's *sharp-intake-of breath* school of depressing theatre-management over the years & although in America the constant injunction to HAVE A NICE DAY & things being perpetually AWESOME can get a bit much.... I just love the energy of people who want to run with a good idea rather than immediately look for drawbacks.....

I look forward to going back to direct at Opera Philadelphia in the New Year... see how the weeks roar by...!

1ˢᵗ October 2017

Today, **Sunday**, I had an SOS call from Jocelyn at about 6pm, asking if I could come down & help her because Mr. C was *'threatening to kill me.'* I was in the middle of cooking family supper - so said I could come down a bit later. After supper I duly did so & peace had broken out by then & Ron was asleep in his room. Had a chat with Jocelyn to check she was alright etc etc....

9ᵗʰ October 2017

Do hope all with you & Emma - sending greetings from the Bedford Hotel in Southampton Row WC1 - I'm here doing some masterclasses on theatre directing with students for the International Schools' Theatre Association at Conway Hall... nice to see new generation of theatre-makers coming on (mad fools!)

30th October 2017

On **Monday** Jocelyn rang to say Ron on very good form & keen to go out. Took him to the Woodspeen where he saw *'that blonde'* on the phone & in a trice his eyesight problems disappeared...)

On **Wednesday** I took Ron & Jocelyn to John Lewis in Newbury to shop for new towels & bed linen. Ron said he'd like to stay out & about & have some lunch - so we went to the Red House in Marsh Benham where Ron moaned about the quality of the fish & chips - but left his plate clean & ate

174

heartily. Thereafter he relished the lemon tart - as you know, Ron's always been a keen advocate of desserts...

Back at the apartment I fitted up Ron's speaker - so now Jocelyn (& later Maria I noticed) can stream music from their phones. I left Ron in the kitchen eating his lunch to the calming strains of Mozart... I then drove to the mobility store and pharmacy in Marlborough for various incontinence-aids & disposable gloves etc.
On **Friday** Ron was sitting on the sofa enjoying listening to some light classical music streamed from Maria's iPhone.

As per my previous email - Ron generally on excellent form this week - much stronger physically - hard to believe he's the same man as the one who often languishes for hours in bed in the morning.... he was so strong that I felt confident enough to take him out on my own on Monday - such was the change in his energy levels. Really good to witness yet another comeback from your dear old dad.... he never ceases to amaze...

12th November 2017

On **Monday,** having consulted with you about the timing of your proposed (& later postponed) Inglewood visit, I took Ron & Jocelyn to the Red House pub in Marsh Benham for lunch. He asked for the roast pork, which came attached to a rather large knuckle-bone & which Jocelyn kindly pounced on & hacked into smaller pieces for him.

...... Jocelyn asked me to get plenty of carnations, because they somehow survive the sweltering central heating in the apartment better than other blooms. I obeyed my instructions. Oh, but the carnation is an ugly, ugly flower, methinks.

On **Wednesday** I had a message in the afternoon from Jocelyn saying that she was having trouble with Mr. C - *'Who was being really nasty today'.* I couldn't get away until my wife was back in the evening & able to take over the childcare & went down at about 6pm. Ron in his bed - though not asleep - so had a little unremarkable (& placid) chat with him. Jocelyn exhausted & reporting that Ron had been shouting at her & berating her all day & he hadn't slept the previous night etc.

A great shame because he's been on much improved form in the last few weeks.

.....Instead of taking Ron out, I took him downstairs to the Inglewood Bistro. I had an idea that Ron might be happier to be installed in his old place by the bar - where he used to sit in the early days with Mr. Brading & speak in elliptical Pinteresque *non-sequiturs* over lunch.... It's certainly lighter there, where he can see out to the gardens & terrace & clock-tower & a far better situation than being in the restaurant facing the brightly-coloured mural-wallpaper - (which, for all it's vivid hues, is still just a wall, rather than a window...)

Ron said he clearly recalled *rolling down the grassy banks* of Inglewood's terraced garden, *'in the early days....'* (When this might have happened is a mystery... I'm not sure it was a recreation Mr. Brading & he were quite agile enough to indulge in, even when they first arrived under Inglewood's exorbitant auspices, all those decades ago...)

Ron seemed chirpy at the prospect of a large-windowed view & enthusiastically ordered sirloin steak & chips - despite my warning that, not being the finest fillet, it might be a bit too chewy - which it duly was & pushed to the side of his plate after much tetchy & ineffective mastication....

Mr. Angus S.B. (a cartoon Anglo-Scottish Aristocrat out of *Cartoon Scottish Aristocrat Central Casting,* Edinburgh) sat at the next door table, grumpily banging on about Brexit & the useless Theresa May & berating the bistro kitchen for taking an age to deliver his scallops. He huffed and puffed about the latest round of cabinet sackings. I'm afraid I made the mistake of asking why Priti Patel would have set up all those 'holiday' meetings in Israel, without informing her party bosses, implying that it was all a bit fishy & perhaps there might be some sort of cover-up behind her hasty resignation.

Mr. S.B. was not at all keen to imagine there might be any kind of hidden conspiracy behind the headlines of his beloved right-wing press & was decidedly short with me. I

176

think he was probably just hungry. He later apologised & warmly shook my hand on his departure. (Perhaps because he overheard me talking to Ron about having worked at Glyndebourne and the Royal Opera House - though I no-longer have any special access to their box offices, if that's what he was hoping...)

Ron on generally good form that day. Chirpy & happy to be sitting & watching the world go by, even if only through the patio door of Blandy's Bistro.

Alan was down last weekend & cut Ron's hair, I gather/observe. Apparently Alan also cuts Theresa May's hair. So the Prime Minister is in very good company in the tonsorial department, sharing scissor-wielding company with the one & only Ron Clempson...

19th November 2017

On **Monday** cycled down to Inglewood to see Ron who wanted to *'speak to me personally'*. I think at the back of his mind was a worry about Christmas & what he might need to do. I talked him through last year's approach - that he bought various vouchers for his grandchildren & took advice on other gifts (e.g. headphones for Caroline's boys) & he seemed reassured. He was worried that he'd lost the (hair) comb I bought him the previous week.

Then went to Inglewood with children & Claire to deliver shopping & Ron very sweet with kids - lights up when he sees them - enjoying Thomas's tales of playing football & Louisa's of her ballet classes (so far so stereotypical, I'm afraid...) Played Ron Claire's Handel aria from her new CD on his speaker & he very impressed.... BTW - Ron's really enjoying that little bluetooth speaker & listening to lots of 1940s dance bands etc....a good mood changer...

On **Tuesday** went down to Inglewood Bistro with Ron for lunch & other residents made a fuss of him. Usual table in corner by bar so he could watch world go by.

177

26th November

The weather was bright and Ron wanted to go out, so I took him to lunch at the Woodspeen. Patron/Chef John Campbell and the team said how glad they were to see him return.

At lunch, Ron said that he wanted to share with me a secret & told me that he had proposed marriage to Josie but that *'she doesn't want to marry me & says why should we change an arrangement between us that is working perfectly well?'*

Ron seemed sanguine, rather than crestfallen, about this maintenance of the status quo at number 7 & entirely unaware that he might have previously raised this matrimonial topic with me. He enjoyed his lunch (& thankfully I managed to steer him towards choosing a main course that was an uncomplicated fish/mash/pea purée combo & worked well with his somewhat challenged dental capabilities.)

3rd December 2017

On **Tuesday** Ron fancied going out to lunch so we went to The Woodspeen. He had a good time - though asked for some red wine to follow his champagne & didn't like either of the first wines he brought, so at the third attempt they produced an extra-special glass of a wine that they usually only sell by the bottle (& didn't charge him) & Ron declared it fit to drink. He's a most valued customer, you see & the service there is really very good.

On **Thursday** evening passing by & popped in to Inglewood & Ron on good form & warm in his armchair on a cold, cold night.

Tomorrow I'm off to queue at the American Embassy in Grosvenor Square for my interview for my visa to direct at Opera Philadelphia in the New Year. It's a Visa code 01 - for an Alien of Extraordinary Ability (!) - yet again I have to prove, of course, why I should be taking a job away from an American director.

Please tell me I'm not going to be queuing at Embassies post-*Brexshit,* if I want to direct more operas in Europe, having had my European Passport untimely ripped from my poor Bohemian hand...

15th December 2017

On **Monday**, a very cold day, I went to Inglewood to see Ron & was invited to stay for lunch at the Bistro. It really was too cold to take Ron out that day to a pub/restaurant. Later I went to Cobb's Farm near Hungerford to pick up Ron's tree - we were hoping to do it together last week, but he wasn't feeling up to it. I spent £48 on a rather handsome fir & helped Jocelyn set it up. Ron pronounced himself delighted with the Christmas Tree, he'd never seen a finer specimen etc.
I picked up some anti-biotics from Kintbury Surgery & in the early evening, when I returned to deliver them, Ron had unexpectedly taken against the tree. He said he wanted it taken out & burned & that he'd only got it to please Jocelyn, *'poor kid'.*

As an alternative to instant cremation, he suggested that I might be able to take it into the street & sell it. Either way, he wanted rid of the thing.... I said I wouldn't be able to effect this immediately, but would set such a course of action in motion (thus buying myself a bit of time...)

On **Tuesday** I picked up a urine sample from the apartment & delivered it to the GP's surgery. Thankfully, Ron had comprehensively forgotten his former animosity towards the Christmas Tree.

The Woodspeen, in the pre-Christmas rush, was pretty full & Ron was most unhappy with the noise levels. *'Half of these people are, in my opinion, peasants...'* he opined. John Campbell the Patron/Chef & Allessandro the Maitre d' appeared & made a fuss of him. The waiter brought him his favourite wine & didn't charge him for it.

A little later, Ron descended into melancholy... *'I've caused a lot of misery and I'm so sorry...'*

I went round the table & drew up a chair to sit close to him

179

& again we went through that perennial conversation where I have to acquaint him with the sad fact that his parents are no longer with us. *'How long ago did my mother die?'* he asked me, once he'd got over the shock of realising his orphan status. *"I remember her physical warmth, so well. Her arms..."*

He cheered up over a chocolate dessert & thereafter on the way home, sufficient to remember a London address he hasn't mentioned before - 5 Benyon Road - he said he thought it might be in the East End. Then he suggested it might have been his grandparents' house. Or that when the Clempson family home, 73 Ollerton Road was damaged in The Blitz, that the family re-located there. I later looked up the address on streetview - there's a Benyon Road in N1 - but the flats are 1960s brutalist - perhaps built on bomb sites.... But it's always intriguing when your Dad opens up a lost memory-vault...

I made one longer-distance personal journey today, to go to my parents' to look after my tragically taciturn, dementia-suffering father, while my mother went out for the day (in a brief respite from the caring duties that are driving her, in her turn, to distraction.) My horse-loving sister and veterinarian niece took her to The Horse of the Year Show.

Claire has gone to Bilbao tonight. Lucky Claire, lucky Bilbao. In the next 8 days she's singing THE MESSIAH with The Kings Consort in beautiful/historic venues in Spain, Germany, Switzerland, France.

Meanwhile, I am at home & doing my *Superdad Act* for the duration. Wish me luck...

30th December 2017

On **Thursday** 21st popped in to see Ron - he in bed & still pretty weak & his voice dropped from baritone to bass.

On **Christmas Eve** did some shopping at Boots for multi-packs of incontinence wear/baby-wipes/pads/gloves etc. Went to Inglewood to see Ron & took Louisa (6) - who is very good at wrapping presents. Ron up from bed & in his chair & on the mend. Louisa & I wrapped presents for Josie,

Jocelyn & Maria (those tokens) & put them under the Christmas Tree, chatting to Ron the while. He very sweet with little Louisa.

On **Boxing Day** Ron rang on his mobile with Compliments of the Season.

On **Wednesday 27th** Popped in with Felix (16) & Louisa (6) to deliver the cash he'd requested & chatted with Ron (in bed but not too weak).

After that tricky time with Ron in hospital he seems to be much stronger again. Certainly he was chatty yesterday. His voice now going back up the octave again.

I'm in Philadelphia from 11th January to 10th February & then to Nice with kids for half-term (Claire singing at Opera Monte Carlo) & back from 17th February.

Warmest wishes to you & Emma
& every good wish for a Happy New Year!

181

C IS FOR CHEERIO

ME:
(standing) Well, listen, Ron - I'll leave
you to get some kip -
MR. C:
Don't worry about that, dear boy - at any
rate -
ME:
(finding an object) What is this? This is
for whacking people..
MR. C:
No - it's a shoe horn! (they laugh) For
God's sake! (laughter) Only occasionally
for whacking people!
ME:
Yeah, exactly!
MR. C:
Used as a shoe-horn!
ME:
Or for getting whacked! If you're into a
bit of good old British masochism.
MR. C:
It wouldn't have been the first one I've
whacked myself with.
ME:
Miss Whiplash!
MR. C:
Yeah! I bet! I sometimes have anger!
ME:
(going to slightly open window) Listen,
I'll close this for you now - so you don't
get wet.
MR. C:
Yah..

ME:
So you don't get flooded by the rain -
MR. C:
Are you going to be alright? Are you sure?
ME:
Yeah - I'm going to use your car.
MR. C:
Yeah - I know that.
ME:
I'm going to steal your motor yet again!
MR. C:
You wouldn't do anything quite like that!
ME:
I've got the keys to A3 OLD..
MR. C:
Yeah.. well old boy, you drive carefully.
ME:
So I don't have to cycle home, you see.
Thanks to you. 'Cause I'd get soaked in the
downpour - on my bike. I hope you can have
a restful night.
MR. C:
Well, I'll try.
ME:
Think happy thoughts!
MR. C:
Yeah - I will look forward to waking in the
morning -
ME:
Don't let the demons get you!
MR. C:
What?
ME:
Don't let the demons get you..
MR. C:
No.
ME:
If they come for you, just say 'I know I'm
only dreaming. Piss off!'
MR. C:
Yeah - okay, old boy.
ME:
Say, 'I know this is just a dream - get
lost!'

183

MR. C:

I'll do that..

ME:

'I'm not listening to you, you bastards!
You won't get the better of me!'

MR. C:

Okay..

ME:

I'm afraid I've drunk your champagne. I got
you a glass and then drank it myself!

MR. C:

Good!

ME:

That's the kind of freeloading bastard I am,
Ron – what can I say?

MR. C:

You're very kind – thank you! (laughter)
Thank you very much, old boy. I'll see you
sometime tomorrow.

ME:

Absolutely.

MR. C:

You sleep well too.

ME:

Do you want these lights off or on?

MR. C:

Sorry old boy - (moans in discomfort)

ME:

Are you having a cramp? Oh dear, you poor
thing…

MR. C:

No, it's fine – Oh it's my leg – ow! – Oh
God – I'll get over it – don't worry – it's
no - it's a short bed, you see.

ME:

Yeah.. Poor you ..

MR. C:

It's called a Hospital Bed.

ME:

Yeah, absolutely..

MR. C:

… for all the right reasons… but bloody
uncomfortable –

ME:
… Yeah, but I suppose it can make you recline - or -

MR. C:
Well.. yeah - okay -

ME:
Will you manage? Do you want me to turn lights off - or - ?

MR. C:
No - can we turn them off?

ME:
Yeah, sure …. if I can work out how to do it..

MR. C:
If one of the girls was leaving -

ME:
There we go..

MR. C:
She'll turn everything off..

ME:
Absolutely..

MR. C:
Okay, old boy..

ME:
… I've turned the - shall I leave the bathroom light off as well?

MR. C:
Off?

ME:
Yeah.. It's off.

MR. C:
Wonderful.

ME:
Okay.

MR. C:
And I'll see you sometime tomorrow..

ME:
Yeah - give me a ring tomorrow.

MR. C:
Okay - I'll do that.. my schedule..

ME:
Yeah.. it'd be nice.. just check in - absolutely -

MR. C:

Yeah, yeah - just to check in.

ME:

Good to see you, Ron.

MR. C:

Yeah..

ME:

I hope you can get some rest.

MR. C:

Yeah.. shut the door after you, would you,
old boy..

ME:

Absolutely - night-night..

MR. C:

Thank you, *goodnight*...

186

2018

3rd January 2018
To: Graham Clempson
Subject: Driving Mr. C

Dear Graham

I saw your Dad yesterday afternoon & we had a good chat –
he was tired & in bed at 4.30pm but pretty chirpy.

I was in London for meetings & a matinee today so didn't
get to visit on his birthday - but Claire took the kids down to
see Ron this afternoon & gave him a card Louisa had
decorated for him & he sweet & grateful & moved...

10th January 2018

Hello from Philadelphia!

Herewith quick update on those first days of January in
Ronsworld.
In general he was on good form but pretty tired...

On **Thursday 4th** evening I picked up another shopping
list. Delivered the groceries & Ron in bed but interested to
hear about my day (we'd been to the matinee of NETWORK
at National Theatre - Christmas present to my wife who's
obsessed with Bryan Cranston - managed to get tickets to sit
at the *on-stage* restaurant - major Brownie-points earned &
soon spent...)

On **Sunday 7th** I went down to Ron's at 4pm to help
Jocelyn get rid of the Christmas Tree. It was dead & stiff &
needed branches cutting off before I could get it in the lift.
Lacking garden tools, we hacked at it with kitchen scissors
and carving knife. When it arrived it was so green & bouncy

& wrapped in a restraining netting. Twelfth Night had passed & it had to go. Poor tree. Ron very amused to watch our efforts with branches & Henry the Hoover. I took the vacuum cleaner to the lift & entrance hall to tackle the pine needles shed at the tree's departure – in attempt keep on-side with other Inglewood Inmates...

Jocelyn told me that Ron had been saying he wanted her to shoot him & was feeling a little maudlin. I stayed for a cuppa & chatted away to distract him from his melancholia. He was kind and encouraging about the prospect of my trip here to America. Ron's voice pretty much back to normal after that pre-Christmas illness & chest infection - when it seemed to drop from tenor to baritone. His resilience continues to amaze me.

I made two longer-distance personal journeys in this period. The first to Oxford for the play-through of the new opera I'm directing in the summer for Cromarty Youth Opera - a brand new commission called TOD! & based on Beatrix Potter's children's story *The Tale of Mr. Tod.* (I'm hoping to get Aldeburgh Productions interested in it. Benjamin Britten was keen to write it as an opera - but was blocked by copyright problems.) The second personal journey was to Sutton Coldfield (109 miles from Kintbury) to run a workshop for Brummie singers/teachers in a chilly church.

Warmest wishes from Philly - do let me know if you are on the East Coast in mid-February & fancy seeing the show. In Ben Britten's words it's 'nasty modern music' that my Gilbert & Sullivan-loving parents would hate - but I, of course, have grown to love & relish its invention (you can't direct a show if you don't believe in the material). Now I'm nervous about rehearsals starting on Monday. It's my first main-house show in America. A big challenge - but also, of course, a dream-come-true & a real case of *'careful what you wish for'.*

And you can't have **The Excitement** without **The Fear**, methinks....

Gulp/Bring it On..

26ᵗʰ February 2018

On **Wednesday** 21st I went down in the morning for a coffee with Ron. He seems to be in bed all the time at the moment.

Jocelyn asked me to take a box of 'sharps' - syringes & so on - to the GP's surgery for disposal & pick up a new 'sharps bin'.

On **Friday** - Had a cup of tea with Ron. Jocelyn told me that he'd been nasty to her again last week & she'd ended up ringing Caroline. The same tirade about seeing her ugly face EVERYWHERE. (I think that was just because he was delivering his denunciation in front of the bathroom mirrors.) Poor Jocelyn. Poor Ron.

On **Sunday** late-afternoon, the children were on various "play-dates" - so popped in to see Ron & had a nice cup of tea & he was really 'with-it' & listened with great interest to my tales. He was still in bed, though.

Claire is in her last week in Monaco singing at Opera Monte Carlo. (Snow permitting!) I'm going out on Wednesday to see her final show & then carry her bags & bouquets like the Husband of Diva that I am. It's so brilliant to see her having such a good time out there. Since having kids she's had to step back from opera work & do more concert work & she's so enjoyed the dressing-room camaraderie & the laughs etc out there at Opera Monte Carlo. The star is a massive ego-ed Argentinian tenor who has decided to star in the show AND direct it AND design the set.... (*yeah, right* - with a team of skilful assistants who are The Real Artisans, of course).

The chorus are mostly Italian and French - but Claire is one of the ten extra English chorus who have been drafted in to help correct the mangling of the English words... *'hang at open doors the nets, the **corks**'* - becomes *'hang at open doors the nets, the **cocks**'* and the word '***sheets***' invariably becomes '***shits***' in the singing of the continental chorus members.

(I dread to think what Italian natives hear when they come

189

to see MADAM BUTTERFLY sung by an English cast....)

It's great to hear Claire laughing again at work & I do so hope it'll lead to more, as work begets work in all our trades. Also - she had four weeks on her own on the Home Front when I was away at Opera Philly - so it's good for me to be doing my turn at Daddy Day-Care & for her to be enjoying French Riviera Life, free from family & quotidian concerns...

12th March 2018

Do hope all well - not a great deal to report here - Ron really isn't strong enough for outings at the moment - we have our Inglewood chats & he chips in with kindly *non-sequiturs*. I'm afraid we haven't made it out to the Woodspeen for quite a time...

I made two longer-distance personal journeys this week. The first to leave car at Felix's house in Northfields & go to dress rehearsal of Janacek's THE HOUSE OF THE DEAD - updated to a modern prison from Dostoyevsky's gulags - all tattoos & basketball & beatings - at Covent Garden & the second at the weekend, to Haywards Heath for 50th birthday of Louisa's godfather, Father Charles Sargent (the lovely vicar who has lent us his apartment near Newquay for family holidays over the years. He's very unlike conventional priest. He used to run a pub etc..)

13th March 2018

Yes, I'm really pleased that ENTER THE DRAGONS is having such success for Abigail Dooley & Emma Edwards - the brilliant comedy writers/actors who perform it. In recent years Abigail's been through a gruelling divorce & hasn't been on stage in years - so it's particularly gratifying to see her creating this career renaissance & fearlessly donning wig, extra-long comedy arms & joke-shop teeth.

The show seems to have resonated with audiences, won great reviews & an award at the Brighton Festival & playing at the Edinburgh Festival at the Pleasance Theatre through August is a real accolade. Looks like there might be a tour in the autumn too.

I plan to return home from Cromarty (where I'm directing a new kids' opera this year based on Beatrix Potter's TALE OF MR. TOD) via Edinburgh & see the show there. I haven't had a show at the Edinburgh Festival since I directed my old friend Martin Freeman, in the play on which my film is based... (like the protagonist in Dartmoor, the movie is STILL awaiting a release date...)

Theatre, as you know, is a broad church & I'm just really pleased to be able to say that I've had success with a modern opera at Opera Philadelphia - with great reviews for WRITTEN ON SKIN in New York Times & Wall Street Journal - (usually those critics don't leave the Big Apple) & that I'm still keeping my theatre work going & my work with young people.

As you rightly say, it can be feast or famine in The Biz so please, *Thespis & St Cecilia*, bring me a full fridge...

25th March 2018

On **Tuesday** 20th I popped in to see Ron - he was on much better form than recently - listening intently to my tales & chipping in. We had a good chat & a nice cup of tea (Ron was in bed but chirpy) & almost back to his old self. When I delivered the shopping at about 3pm that afternoon, Ron was asleep in bed - as he seems to be much more often these days.

On **Wednesday** I was in Hove for rehearsals of my comedy play ENTER THE DRAGONS and about 5pm had a call from a distressed-sounding Jocelyn, asking if I could come down to Inglewood immediately. Jocelyn said that Ron had punched her in the stomach & that the doctor had been out & paramedics & that the doctor had called the police to be in attendance. I was working in Sussex & not able to help... but I rang nice Ian Crawford to see if he could help. Ian rang Jocelyn & spoke to her & I had a text from her later saying that peace had broken out & all was calm & Ron was asleep.

On **Thursday**.... Josie was there & Ron was asleep. She said that a police officer *had* been in attendance the night before & that Jocelyn had kept the officer away from Ron.

191

Josie was hazy on the details of the previous night's events. I haven't seen Jocelyn since to find out exactly what transpired. Josie said she thought that Jocelyn had kept your sister Caroline informed....

On **Friday** I rang to see if any assistance/shopping was needed & Maria said that she had all the provisions she needed & that all was well. It didn't sound like there had been any recurrence of Wednesday evening's turbulence. I will of course let you know more as I know it.

3rd April 2018

Claire's singing tomorrow night in the London Handel Festival at St George's Hanover Square (Handel's own church) - she's rehearsing now & battling the nerves... she'll be great, of course, but somehow you can't have the excitement without the fear - well it must be like that for Emma on live TV! - you must know all about being married to a performer...

8th April 2018

I was working in London Tuesday to Saturday this week with British Youth Opera. (Fantastic young singers who might just rescue opera from The Diva Dinosaurs - but some are still being taught by old-fashioned former-stars who hark back to a time where opera acting was terrible...)

Today I popped in to see Ron in the morning - District Nurse there doing his injection etc - he was up in his chair in the sitting room.

This **Tuesday** is my Godmother's funeral in Stowmarket & so I'm going to Suffolk tomorrow
& tying in some research at the Britten-Pears Library in Aldeburgh & a meeting - pitching for a new production at Snape Maltings/Aldeburgh Festival... & then on to Ipswich crematorium/Stowmarket church from there the next morning... daffodils & funerals... & spring is finally here....
& our hemisphere tilts back to the sun again...

22nd April 2018

On **Monday** popped in & helped Maria get Ron out of bed & thereafter into his chair - had a coffee with him & chatted.

On **Thursday** - popped in to apartment - Ron sitting at kitchen table having his lunch, pleased that the sun was shining. Jocelyn took him out in his wheelchair for some fresh air that day, I gather. He's really not yet strong enough yet for a spin in A3 OLD, I'm afraid...

I made one longer-distance personal journey to my son Felix's house in Ealing - left the car there & went on in to town & Young Vic where I saw the excellent THE INHERITANCE - two part marathon play (pm & eve sessions) that's received well-deserved rave reviews. Another gay odyssey a little bit like ANGELS IN AMERICA - but this time based on EM Forster's HOWARD'S END... hard to explain but a terrific ensemble piece.... I think it's bound to transfer to the West End & thereafter NYC, I don't doubt...

29th April 2018

On **Friday** went down about 2pm & pleasingly found Ron on excellent form - sitting up in his chair & chatting - much more vocal than he's been for a while & talking about his plans to take on 'The Council' (?!) & to help his kids & that it would be good to convene a meeting of the Committee Members (?!) to talk through Annual Results etc... almost back to his previously more dynamic (but somewhat surreal) self - really nice to see. When I returned to deliver the groceries early evening - I was delighted to see Ron sitting up in his chair & enjoying the racing from Chepstow on the telly - we had a chat about runners & riders....

....into town by tube for meeting at the Finsbury Park studio of the designer of my Cromarty show this year - based on Beatrix Potter's TALE OF MR. TOD. How the heck are we going to do little baby rabbits trapped in an oven at Mr. Tod's foxy burrow *and* have them sing & be heard?? We'll have to find a way..

7th May 2018

Writing this from the train on the way back from the Eden Project in Cornwall - where I've been running a theatre project for ISTA (International Schools' Theatre Association) with 100 kids from schools all around the world.... Paris, Berlin, Istanbul etc - (& also from the American International School in gloriously exotic Egham...)

As I make my long journey eastwards, everyone else with a normal job in Kintbury is at home for the Bank Holiday weekend & cremating sausages on barbecues & watching their darlings skipping around the Maypole at the Coronation Hall & wowing to the incredible antics of our local troupe of geriatric, hankie-waving Morris Dancers.

But I shall have the last laugh when, tomorrow morning, the PAYE dads are back on the 06.23 train to their stuffy London offices & I am free (post-school run) to have a leisurely coffee in my little garden... self-employment has to have the odd perk...

9th May 2018

Had a cup of tea together - Ron in bed but listening well & contributing well to our chat.... told him about my work at the Eden Project & Thomas's tenth birthday this weekend etc... he sweetly joining in *'Bless you, bless you'*... weak of course, but alert. Josie told me that he had another mini-stroke while I was away & was unwell - but no evidence today of any specific impairment. He really is amazingly strong to withstand such setbacks.

13th May 2018

On **Wednesday** I tracked down some strawberries at Tesco & delivered early for breakfast. Had a nice hour with Ron who was on good form. Told him about my adventures in Cornwall & of my son Thomas's imminent birthday celebrations (he was 10 yesterday & we took him to the world's classiest bowling alley with 9 of his school-friends. Luckily kids have questionable/little taste & they seemed to think it was the Valhalla of Amusement Parks... & relished the nutritionally negligible yellow foodstuffs...) Ron engaged & listening to my stories & laughing. Good to see.

On **Thursday** morning at 8.30am I had the following plaintive text from Josie:

"Hi Will, could you please spare me 5 mins? Mr. C is being awkward and I'm struggling just to transfer him into his reclining chair."

I told Josie I'd be down as soon as I'd done the school run. Turned up at 9.05am - but Ron had obviously become compliant - as he was sitting in happily in his chair in the sitting room. I had coffee with Ron & then set off to see my own father (& his carer, my mother) who has his own struggles with dementia etc... (oh, the common challenges for all our families.. & on and on for our progeny as the population progressively ages...)

On **Saturday** I went to Inglewood to collect a list for the mobility store in Marlborough & drove over there to pick up various incontinence equipment & protective gloves.

I made one longer-distance journey, to my parents' house in Hanworth (56 miles from Kintbury) and left the car there while I went to see MAYFLY at the Orange Tree Theatre, Richmond & then in the evening to see LESSONS IN LOVE AND VIOLENCE the new opera by Sir George Benjamin (I directed his WRITTEN ON SKIN in Philadelphia - so, politically very important to be seen & to crash the after-premiere-party & tell the composer how much I adored it etc etc...)

This week, from Wednesday to Friday, I'm up in the Highlands - in Cromarty for meetings re. this year's children's opera.

15th May 2018

Thank you so much for your kind words. If I were living far from my Dad I'm sure I'd like it if there were some local who could look out for him & it's a privilege to be thus entrusted.

Popped in to see Ron yesterday & although abed, he was on

good-humoured form - regaled him with tales of Thomas's bowling alley birthday - though poor Ron had had overnight tummy trouble. Josie sent me off to the dry cleaners & Tesco & to get some *Immodium*....

3ʳᵈ June 2018

Not a great deal to report this week - I was away with the kids in Devon for half-term, Monday to Thursday & then on Friday rehearsing with B'Opera (making an opera for the under-2s!) in Birmingham.

Yesterday, **Saturday**, I went down to see Ron in the afternoon. He was in bed - but we had a good chat & he was animated in his responses & enjoyed my tales of sailing up the River Dart from Dartmouth (in a friend's boat!) with the children on a fine Bank Holiday Monday & playing for high stakes in the penny arcade on Teignmouth Pier in the rain the day after. Ron asleep when I returned to Inglewood later.

4ᵗʰ June 2018

Just popped in to see Ron & pick up shopping list from J&J. He was in bed but on good form & we had a cuppa together & he was very happy to have seen you yesterday & said you gave him an excellent report of the company's financial results & that all his investments are doing well under your expert care...

10ᵗʰ June 2018

On **Tuesday** I cycled down to Inglewood about 2pm & Jocelyn said that the District Nurse
had come to give Ron his injection - but that he'd rejected her & refused to comply & so she'd gone away & said she'd return later. He was actually on rather good form when I chatted with him - we talked through his busy children's lives & all their exciting globe-trotting... Later learned that the District Nurse had returned & Ron had forgotten his earlier objections to her ministrations & all was well.

I made one personal longer-distance journey, on Friday - to the opening night of the Aldeburgh Festival - a terrific concert, then a not-so-hot new opera...

I love going to Aldeburgh
& the Benjamin Britten connections
& had the most delicious fish & chips sitting on the shingle
under the beady eyes of opportunist seagulls..

July 1st 2018

On **Tuesday** picked up a vomit-stained blanket from a tired & tearful Josie - poor Ron had been sick in the night & she was exhausted. I took said blanket to Swift Cleaners in Hungerford. Ron was awake but feeling weak. Exchanged a few words but didn't want to tire him further.

On **Wednesday** morning, as per a request from Josie, I withdrew £100 from ATM for Ron's wallet & took it to Inglewood. The chiropodist was coming that day & money needed for payment. Later in the day it transpired that it was an NHS rather than a private chiropodist who visited Ron & so no cash needed to be handed over.

Jocelyn asked me if I'd stay while she shaved Ron - so that I could help her move him up the bed etc - but he'd fallen fast asleep after eating some breakfast. I returned after lunch & Jocelyn gave Ron his shave & a wash etc & then I stayed & had a cuppa with him & we had a perfectly sensible & kindly chat.

I made two longer-distance personal journeys this week - the first to Edgbaston for a rehearsal of Baby Opera Company - I'm helping them devise their new show for babies & toddlers - called ANIMAL MAGIC, featuring doctored opera excerpts & nursery rhymes etc. Good to get them young!

My second trip was to visit my own father in Hanworth, Middlesex. Left the car at his house & took Uber taxis to Richmond to see Rupert Everett's new film about Oscar Wilde - THE HAPPY PRINCE. A film that Rupert has been trying to make for years & years & had his funding collapse at the last minute several times. He plays Oscar Wilde & writes & directs the film. A really good effort & a labour of love.

Maggie says she knows *Roops* because his mother lives next door to her (Pewsey?) Mill where she lived with John (post-Ron husband) & she once went to the house for Christmas lunch & Rupert was perfectly charming. He's certainly a good actor & rather a good writer. His scandalous showbiz memoirs (*Red Carpets & other Banana Skins & The Vanished Years*) are, I must say, written in a really excellent prose style.

I was glad to take my Dad out that day & despite *his* dementia he seemed to really enjoy it - (he's just three years younger than your old man). He hasn't been to the cinema for many years. Oscar Wilde has always been a mutual fascination for us both & when I saw the movie had been released, I really wanted to take him to see it, rather than waiting for the DVD.

Poor Oscar. I can't pass through Reading station without looking out & thinking of him languishing at that horrible jail. It was briefly open to the public last year for an art installation - it ceased to be a working prison in 2013. It was so moving to sit in the prison chapel & in Wilde's cell & think of a genius much abused. And, of course, to think of him at Clapham Junction being abused and spat at by passing members of the public, as he waited, in his prison garb, to change trains. (This horrid scene is artfully recreated in the movie.) Again: poor old Oscar...

Anyway - I'll pop in tomorrow to see how things are at Inglewood.

Ron is in a decline, of course, but still packs the odd unexpected right hook or *King Lear*-like categorical objection to some prosaic procedure - but, as you know, he can also grace us with a timely *bon mot* or beaming smile & an intense gratefulness - *'Bless you, thank you, Bless you,'* he'll say, when in a gentler mood..

2ⁿᵈ July 2018

Just popped in to see your Dad - this pm - asleep but calm & comfortable - Jocelyn asked me to get him a vitamin drink called *Ensure Plus* she wants to try - he's not been eating

last couple of days & it's a way to give him some nutrients...
just picked some up at Newbury Boots - chocolate or banana
flavours to see if he will take them...

Dear old Ron....

****

8th July 2018
Subject: Farewell Mr. C

Dear Graham

My deepest condolences to you and all the family.

Thank you for the privilege of the past four-and-a-half
years, knowing Ron & for making possible all our
adventures...
He was one of a kind & I was lucky to get to know him.

Herewith an update on this final, momentous week.

On **Monday** I went to Inglewood in the morning & picked
up a shopping list from Jocelyn.
Ron was not able to eat, but Jocelyn suggested I buy some
special vitamin drinks (& toiletries) from Boots.

When I got back to Inglewood I had (what turned out to be
my last) chat with Ron. Talked about the weather outside &
that it was the kind of climate he loved - beach weather & I
talked about his holidays in Barbados & the Cote d'Azur -
with Ron very much understanding & agreeing.

On **Friday** I went to visit Ron after school drop-off at
9.15am. Jocelyn and Josie were with him & Josie had been
up with him since 12.30am. He was beginning his final
journey. I held his hand & spoke & tried to reassure him
that all was well. He was not able to respond vocally, but
held tightly onto my hand, as he did to Josie and Jocelyn's.

As I left at 10.45am, Sarah Jane had just arrived.

True to form, I went to Tesco with a last shopping list, to
buy wet-wipes & toilet roll & flowers.

199

I delivered the shopping later, returned Ron's debit card to his wallet & met Caroline for the first time. Many times we've almost met. Good to finally meet her, but in sad circumstances.

I went to see Ron & when his breathing became laboured, made myself scarce, so he was with his family for his final hours. I picked up Alex at Kintbury Station at 3.10pm & brought him to Inglewood to see Ron. I asked Caroline if Andrew would need collection from the airport - but she said he was sorted for transport.

I left about 4pm & drove to London to see my elder son Felix's school show in Acton. When I arrived at 6pm, I received your voicemail and text messages from Alex and Jocelyn to tell me that Ron had just departed.

I rang & spoke to you in America. Thank you, as ever, for your kind words.

This morning, **Sunday**, I saw Maggie again today who is in a bit of a daze. Says she can't believe Ron's gone. Of course it will take a while for this to sink in for all of us.

Please let me know if I can help with the sale of A3 OLD now that Ron has gone off to ride in a more Ethereal Chariot on the Far Shores.

Thanks again for your terrific generosity to me & my family over the past years.

What a ride it's been...

Do let me know how I can help with moving etc this week. I'm around & at your service. When you know more about Ron's funeral & if it is likely to be one to which friends are invited as well as family, please let me know. I am going to start work in Cromarty on 24th July but am keen to come back 'down south' to attend Ron's funeral, if appropriate.

15th July 2018

On **Friday** I went down to Inglewood to pick up Ron's

clothes for his Final Journey. I drove to the undertaker in Newbury & gave instructions for the inclusion of Ron's photograph of his mother and that famous blue & white shirt he wore to all your weddings. The photograph had to be removed from its frame because anything glass is not permitted in the coffin, pre-cremation.

Today, **Sunday**, Louisa & I have been removing the charity clothes donation boxes from Ron's bedroom. Charity shops are not open today - but I will investigate & distribute next week. As you predicted, books are harder to get someone to take & sorry, but being a great weakling, too heavy for me to carry. (I usually just cry *'stage management!'* when faced with any sort of heavy lifting.)

22nd July 2018

Dear Team Clempson

Just to let you know that the ladies at the Red Cross charity shop in Hungerford were delighted with the donation of those six boxes of Ron's clothes & tremendously grateful. I was working at British Youth Opera in London last week & Mrs K. singing in Belfast so didn't get a chance to make the delivery sooner. Sorry it wasn't an Alzheimer's/Dementia Charity - but researching this I found out that they don't have any high street charity shops any more.

Thank you all very much for the gifts of furniture etc for my family - very much appreciated. Ron's bookshelf is now next to our piano & our musical scores have an excellent new home! I'm sure he'd be pleased to see it *in situ*. The television is tremendous! A thousand thanks. We will never forget Ron & his kindness & all of yours over the last five years.

16th August 2018

Dear Team Clempson

Forgive the rather impersonal, cyber *Thank-You Card,* but since there's such a wide, globe-trotting diaspora of the Clempson clan, it's the only way to reach you all at once....

201

Thank you SO MUCH for inviting & including me in that very moving Memorial Lunch for Ron.
It was a fitting tribute & so thoughtfully created & presented.

The only one missing was Ron,
who so loved a good lunch in excellent company...

Warmest wishes to you all

WK

p.s. Over the years, Ron was always so kind to my family - as you have all been & for which I'm eternally grateful.

Here's a pic of Ron with my boy Thomas,
a couple of years ago,
when we took him to a Classic Car Rally in a village nearby.
Ron loved seeing the vintage motors
& sharing a cream tea
& it's a memory of a good day out with your Dad
& makes me think of him enjoying whatever is the car's celestial counterpart
over there on the Elysian Fields...

A Silver Cloud, perhaps?

Epilogue

And so ended the days when I was lucky enough to be DRIVING MR. C.   What began as a small *side-hustle* to supplement my inconsistent theatrical earnings - something I initially saw as representative of my financial failure - soon became a real pleasure, a valuable life-lesson: a shortfall turned into a characterful stroke of good fortune.

I wasn't to know, in July 2018, when I said my final farewell to Ron, that there was soon to be a major bereavement in my own family.   Within a year, my mother died unexpectedly, shortly after her eightieth birthday - diagnosed with an inoperable brain tumour in March 2019 and dead only three months later.   The previous Christmas, as Mum's treat to us all, the whole family - children, spouses and grandchildren - went together to the pantomime at Richmond Theatre.   All of us were concerned for our frail father's welfare on that excursion on a cold December day – with no notion that my mother was unwell.   But within six months, it was she who was gone.

It was a horrid, cruel, descent – and a shockingly swift one. My sisters and I never expected my mother to pre-decease my dementia-suffering father.   Poor Mum always had a dream that once Dad had departed, and she was able to relinquish her more recent, demanding role as his carer, she'd return to her rural roots and live with my younger sister in Sussex. Alas - it was not to be.

But all our lives are full of unexpected twists and turns, highs and lows.

The five years I drove Ron were a real blessing.   His family were generous and unfailingly kind to me and my family. Real treasure in life can come from simply being trusted. Ron was a true old-school eccentric, life-loving, characterful, cantankerous, difficult, deluded – but he was absolutely one-of-a-kind.   It was always a good day if I could crack a corny joke that had him laughing - he'd throw his head back and roar, *'I LOVE IT!'* He is much missed by family, of course, but also by all of us whose lives he touched with his incorrigible opinions and his irrepressible vitality. His voice is still loud and distinct in my head. *'Dear boy, come on in!'* he'd cry as I knocked and let myself into his apartment, calling his name, wondering what would be our latest escapade.

My father has accomplished the move from home that my mother longed for. *He* now lives with my patient and caring younger sister in Sussex. As I write, we are in the midst of the laborious process of clearing and selling our parents' house – a home they had for more than half-a-century. I first arrived there as a three-week-old baby. We've found the memorabilia Mum hoarded, piles of our childhood birthday cards, old school uniforms, the love-letters she exchanged with my father in their 'courting' days.

I'm emptying my father's study of his beloved books. Each time I trudge downstairs, carting away another hefty cardboard box, I still expect my mother to be in her armchair watching television, or bustling around in her small kitchen at the rear of the house, offering cheese-on-toast, cups of tea and dubious opinions harvested from the *Daily Express.*

My brilliant mentor Jonathan Miller died just a few months after my mother. I was very lucky to know him, too. His genius lives on in memorable recordings of his productions, broadcasts and interviews. He gave me many of his books and we have several of the abstract collages he created on the walls of our home – one given as our wedding present. Our departed family and friends are always with us, their faces lit up in our eyes, their voices echoing on in our ears - for as long as *our* memories work. Even if you don't believe in anything beyond the grave, that's an afterlife of reminiscence we're all bequeathed.

****

Despite Ron's departure, thanks to his family, I still get to drive A3 OLD, Mr. C's beloved Audi. His son Graham covers motor insurance and his daughter Sarah funds the car's running costs. Mrs Sharp – Maggie - Ron's second wife who features in these pages, still lives at Inglewood and has recently, quite sensibly, decided it's time to give up driving. And so, when I'm not away from home rehearsing, I happily take Maggie to Waitrose once a week, to visit her old friends and former neighbours in Henley-on-Thames, to medical or dental appointments, to visit family in Hampshire and London. Each week I send an email to Graham's younger half-siblings, Sarah and Alex, the children Maggie had with Ron, letting them know of my adventures with Mrs Sharp.

So I may not be DRIVING MR. C. any longer –
but here I am, living a new chapter and –
DRIVING MRS S...

Kintbury, Berkshire – June 2020

205

Acknowledgements

With grateful thanks to:

Mr. C's son Graham, to whom this correspondence was addressed.
Mr. C's other children - Sarah, Alex, Caroline and Andrew.
Mr. C's daughter-in-law, Emma.
Mr. C's granddaughter Lily – who created the first version of this book.
Mr. C's ex-wife Maggie.
Mr. C's amazingly patient and long-suffering carers – Jocelyn, Josie, Maria and Nida.

Our kind neighbour Kate Russell – who first told me that Mr. C was seeking a driver.

My understudy driver - Ian Crawford.

Encouraging early readers – Joe Richards, Abigail Dooley, William Miller, Sunetra Sarker, Edward Caswell, Harry Sever, James Kerr and - for his particular encouragement - Scott Carey.

Taragh Bissett for the book-cover design.

Amy Rosenthal – for first telling me that moving story of her writer father Jack, waiting at home for his builder.

My children - Felix, Thomas and Louisa - who soon learned to speak very loudly in conversation with Mr. C.

My wife Claire - for, on a regular basis for the last twenty years, saving my life.

William Kerley is an award-winning director of opera, theatre and film. For five years he was Resident Stage Director at Maestro Lorin Maazel's Castleton Festival in Virginia, U.S.A. His work includes the first new U.S. production of George Benjamin's *Written on Skin* for Opera Philadelphia, the Chinese premiere of *Il Barbiere di Siviglia* at the NCPA in Beijing, China, *La Boheme* at the ROH in Muscat, Oman and the fiftieth anniversary production of Britten's *Gloriana* at the Aldeburgh Festival. His theatre work includes the world premieres of Gill Adams' *Jump to Cow Heaven*, starring Martin Freeman and Richard Bean's *The God Botherers* starring Sunetra Sarker and David Oyelowo. His first feature film *The Krays – Mad Axeman* was released in the U.K. in 2019 and, as *The London Mob,* in the U.S.A. in 2020.

www.willkerley.com

Printed in Great Britain
by Amazon